DAN COHN-SHERBOK

Rabbi Professor Dan Cohn-Sherbok is
one of the world's leading authorities on
Judaism. He has written and edited over
70 books including *Dictionary of Jewish
Biography*, *Fifty Key Jewish Thinkers* and
The Vision of Judaism. He is Professor of
Jewish Theology at the University of
Wales at Lampeter.

THE PARADOX OF ANTI-SEMITISM

THE PARADOX OF ANTI-SEMITISM

DAN COHN-SHERBOK

continuum
LONDON • NEW YORK

Continuum International Publishing Group

The Tower Building   80 Maiden Lane
11 York Road   Suite 704
London SE1 7NX   New York
                               NY 10038

www.continuumbooks.com

First published 2006

British Library Cataloguing-in-Publication Data
A catalogue record for this book is available from the British Library.

ISBN 0–8264–8896–X

Typeset by Fakenham Photosetting Limited, Fakenham, Norfolk
Printed and bound in Great Britain by MPG Books, Bodmin, Cornwall

for Lavinia

CONTENTS

PREFACE

Growing up in the leafy suburbs of Denver, Colorado in the 1950s, I was conscious that Jews were not welcome in the highest levels of Denver society. There was a distinct upper class in my hometown. Gentile WASPs (White Anglo-Saxon Protestants) ruled the city. They were members of the Denver Country Club and the University Club which admitted neither Jews, nor blacks. The Debutante Ball – sponsored by the Denver Symphony – was the highlight of the social season. There had never been a Jewish debutante, and Jews were not welcome at debutante parties. The conductor of the Denver Symphony was himself a Jew, but he was simply tolerated by the non-Jewish establishment.

In my final year at high school, a disturbing experience highlighted the Jewish predicament. I went out with the daughter of one of the most prominent Gentile families who lived in the best area of the city. They belonged to the Denver Country Club. Their house was built in mock-Georgian style; surrounded by acres of lawn, it had a tennis court in the backyard as well as a swimming pool. After we had gone to the movies, this girl suggested we have a drink at her parents' club, assuring me I could go as her guest. By this time, I had my own car, and so we drove there. Apprehensively, I went inside. The club was full of well-dressed, affluent adults as well as a few teenagers.

'You know,' I said, 'I've never been here. It's quite a place.'

'You mean your parents don't belong to a country club?' she asked.

'No. Not even the Jewish country club.'

'Why not?'

'Well,' I said, 'my father doesn't play golf. And my mother doesn't like swimming. So I don't think they thought there would be any point.'

'But you'd like it, wouldn't you?'

'I think I would. But to be honest, I'd rather be a member here.'

'I don't think that would be possible. It's ridiculous, but they don't take Jews, or blacks. I can't see why.'

Here was a real barrier. No matter what I could achieve at high school, where I went to college notwithstanding, such a club would always be out of bounds. No Jews! The American dream stopped at the entrance to this elegant upper-class world. America is, in theory, a classless society. My high school was based on meritocratic principles. But in the outside world real limits to social advancement existed.

Over the last few decades, there has been enormous social change. Today Jews have at long last achieved both civil and social acceptance. No longer are they excluded from exclusive social clubs, or restricted from living in the best areas. Exclusive private schools are filled with Jewish students, and intermarriage is commonplace. Such social integration has been the aspiration of Jews from the time of the Enlightenment in the nineteenth century. Instead of being hated, Jews have now blended into the communities where they live.

Throughout the world Jews have embraced such an alteration in status. In the shadow of the Holocaust, the Jewish world views social toleration as a primary goal. Today Jewry is united in the belief that we must survive. The State of Israel is perceived as an insurance policy against any future attempt to annihilate the Jews. Jewish leaders champion legislation to protect the civil rights of all, knowing that by protecting others we are protecting ourselves. The Jewish Defamation League is ever vigilant about any form of anti-Semitism.

Anti-Semitism, we believe, must be crushed whatever its form. It is a cancer in the body of society that must be eradicated. Any attack on Jews or Israel is regarded as a grave danger. We should celebrate these changes, and rejoice in the opportunities offered by contemporary society. Yet, it must be recognized that in the past anti-Semitism has frequently led to the enrichment of the Jewish heritage. Through the ages, discrimination and persecution intensified the Jewish determination to rely on God and live in accordance with the covenant.

It is a paradox that in modern times the more we have assimilated, the more we have distanced ourselves from the Jewish heritage. With the exception of the ultra-Orthodox, most Jews today are largely ignorant of traditional Jewish values. We do not accept the central principles of the faith. We do not observe the 613 commandments in scripture. We have forsaken the oral *Torah*. For many, the State of Israel has replaced a belief in God as the fulcrum of Jewish existence. In the pursuit of toleration and social acceptance, we have lost hold of the Jewish past.

Rather than being our most ferocious enemy, anti-Semitism has, I believe, often fostered Jewish survival. The aim of this study is to demonstrate the ways in which hostility towards Judaism and the Jewish people has isolated us as a nation and intensified our determination to survive. The more the outside world hated us, the more we relied on God to save us. In the face of violence, we sacrificed ourselves to sanctify his name. Through over three millennia, we have seen ourselves as God's suffering servants. Our mission has been to serve God and advance his kingdom. We have been God's chosen people, whose destiny is to witness his eternal truth.

This, however, has not been the vision of Jewish modernists. Alongside assimilationists who have pressed for acceptance through social integration, Zionists have sought to overcome prejudice through the creation of a Jewish commonwealth in the Holy Land. At the end of the nineteenth century, secular Zionists argued that anti-Semitism is an insurmountable evil. In their view, there is no escape. In *Rome and Jerusalem*, the German secular

Zionist Moses Hess argued that anti-Jewish sentiment is unavoidable. For Hess, Jews will always remain strangers among the nations; nothing can alter such a situation. The only solution to the problem of Jew-hatred is for the Jewish people to come to terms with their national identity. Similarly, the Russian thinker Leon Pinsker maintained in *Autoemancipation* that Jews are unassimilable and therefore inevitably aliens. The Jewish people, he stated, is everywhere a guest, and nowhere at home. In *The Jewish State* Theodor Herzl similarly viewed anti-Semitism as an inevitable curse. Old prejudices, he believed, are ingrained in western society. For these Zionist thinkers, there is no solution for the ills that beset the Jewish nation: the only remedy for the malady of Jew-hatred is the creation of a Jewish state.

Zionists and assimilationists have thus been united in their denunciation of anti-Semitism. Jew-hatred, they maintain, is a scourge that must be overcome either through Jewish isolationism or integration. Of course anti-Semitism is an evil. But it is a misapprehension to believe that the persistence of Jew-hatred has only had a negative impact on Jewish life. On the contrary, what modern Jews have failed to grasp are the positive benefits of anti-Jewish hostility. It has frequently been the case that contempt for the Jew has united the Jewish people, and forced them to turn inwards. Shunning the attractions of the Gentile world, they have drawn together in their determination to endure and flourish. Through centuries of persecution and massacre, Jews remained faithful to their ancient tradition. It is a delusion to believe that the elimination of Jew-hatred by itself will save the Jewish people. The paradox of Jewish life is that hatred and Jewish survival have been interrelated for thousands of years, and that without anti-Semitism, we may be doomed to extinction.

INTRODUCTION

Currently I am a professor of Jewish Theology at the University of Wales, a small liberal arts university in West Wales. The university is located in Lampeter, a tiny Welsh town surrounded by green hills. My wife and I and our two cats live in an old coach house in the Welsh countryside. Our nearest neighbours are sheep. They have no interest in my religious views. Neither do the few Jews who live in the area. Hence I will not be besieged by either our neighbours or the local Jewish community for arguing that anti-Semitism and Jewish survival are interrelated.

My students are equally unperturbed by my opinions. Recently in an Introduction to Judaism course I told them that I was writing a new book about anti-Semitism. Today, I explained, Judaism is in chaos. No longer are Jews bound by the religious traditions of the past. All this, I went on, is the result of assimilation. In the past Jews were subject to prejudice and discrimination. Lacking social and economic opportunities, they were isolated from the outside world. The Enlightenment changed all that. Jews have gained civil and social equality and, as a result, have largely abandoned the Jewish heritage. What is missing in contemporary society is Jew-hatred. Without such prejudice, I explained, it is difficult to see how the Jewish people will return to their ancient traditions.

My students wrote all this down in their notebooks without a murmur. But at the end of the lecture, one of the students, a curvaceous blonde with a tattoo on her arm, put up her hand. 'Rabbi Dan,' she said with a puzzled expression. 'I don't get it. I just did your Holocaust course, and you said that the Nazis created a racial state. They wanted to kill all Jews. If they'd succeeded, there wouldn't be any Jews left. How can anti-Semitism be a good thing?' In reply, I stressed that I was in no way endorsing genocide, nor was I encouraging hatred of the Jewish people. My only point was that in the past Jewish survival and Jew-hatred have been interconnected. In the modern world, it may be that the absence of such contempt, which drove Jews inward, may paradoxically lead to the disintegration of the Jewish heritage.

My answer caused a degree of consternation, but my student wrote down what I said and asked no further questions. In Wales I am safe from criticism. But this will not be so in the Jewish world. I know it will cause outrage to view anti-Semitism in positive terms, no matter what the reason. I have been a rabbi on four continents and am used to Jewish sensitivities. For understandable reasons Jews have welcomed the opportunities offered by the Enlightenment, and do not wish to return to a ghetto existence. They do not desire to suffer discrimination or persecution, even if the Jewish heritage is at stake. Instead, they are determined to live a comfortable existence, secure and protected.

As a Reform rabbi, I am familiar with the affluent,

assimilated lifestyle of middle-class Jews. The congregations I served after I was ordained were representative
of communities everywhere. A typical example was
the President of Temple Beth-El in a small town in
Pennsylvania where I was a summer rabbi. I can imagine
what his reaction would have been if I had told him
that anti-Semitism can have positive benefits. Even if I
explained to him the ways in which prejudice motivated
Jews to preserve their heritage, he wouldn't listen. He
would get angry. He would threaten me. He would call
me an anti-Semite.

This is just the reaction I had when I discussed my
book with an old friend, Rabbi Brian Fox, who had
been my classmate at the Hebrew Union College over
30 years ago. Currently he is the rabbi of a synagogue
in Manchester. I thought I ought to gauge what my
rabbinical colleagues might say. One evening I reached
him at home and told him that I wanted to discuss my
theory about Jew-hatred. After a brief explanation, he
grunted. 'That's the most ridiculous thing I think I've
ever heard,' he said.

'You mean you don't agree.'

'Agree! How could I possibly agree?'

'But, look, Brian,' I continued. 'I think you've missed the
point. Of course anti-Semitism should be condemned.
Being targeted by Jew-haters is an evil. But if you look
back over Jewish history, I think you'll agree that our
people did not just cave in. In the face of oppression,

Jews embraced the traditions of our people and were determined to live Jewish lives no matter what the cost. They did not give in to our enemies; instead they flourished under the most adverse conditions. Anti-Semitism made them more determined and resolute.'

Of course, in the past there have been periods when Jews were relatively secure and there was an efflorescence of Jewish culture. During the Golden Age of Spain, for example, Jews prospered under Muslim rule. In such a milieu, Jewish civilization flourished. Cordova, the capital of the Ummayad caliphate, became a vibrant centre of Jewish culture attracting poets, grammarians and *yeshivah* students from throughout the diaspora. During the twelfth century biblical commentators, theologians and rabbinic authorities made major contributions to Jewish learning.

Although there were such periods of religious vibrancy in a relatively peaceful environment, these periods of calm were exceptions. In addition, they were invariably interrupted by anti-Jewish outbreaks. At the end of the eleventh century, for example, Spanish Jewish life was disrupted when the Almoravides from North Africa were invited to Spain to lead an attack on Christian communities in the north and persecuted the Jewish community as well. A century later, the golden age of Spain came to an end when the Almohades, a Berber dynasty from Morocco, came to defend the country and simultaneously persecuted the Jewish community. Jews were forced to convert to Islam and academies and synagogues were closed.

It would be a mistake to argue that Jewish religious intensity cannot exist unless Jews are persecuted – this was clearly not invariably the case. The point is rather that contempt for the Jew has in fact had positive benefits. Throughout Jewish history, antipathy towards Jewry has paradoxically reinvigorated Jewish life, and driven Jews back to their ancient traditions. Anti-Semitism is an evil: this is undeniable. The community should make every effort to thwart any form of racial hatred. But, at the same time, we should acknowledge that Jewish survival and Jew-hatred are paradoxically interrelated, and that without anti-Semitism, Jews may not be able to withstand the pressures of the modern world.

The first part of this book outlines the changes that have taken place in the Jewish community since the late eighteenth century. Since the period of the Enlightenment, Jews have sought to ameliorate adverse conditions through integration and assimilation. Escaping from a ghetto existence, modern Jewry has largely overcome prejudice and persecution. In a post-Holocaust age, they have reached the highest levels of society and have made major contributions to the communities in which they reside. Yet, paradoxically, as anti-Semitism has diminished, the traditional Jewish way of life has disintegrated. In its place, Jews have created new forms of the Jewish religion which are radical departures from the past. Living in a tolerant age, modern Jews have largely distanced themselves from their ancient heritage. Without the limitations imposed by anti-Semitic attitudes, they have freed themselves from the religious restrictions of the past.

The book begins in Chapter 1 with a discussion of the nature of traditional Judaism. Here the central tenets of the faith are outlined in detail. Through the centuries,

Jews believed in one God who created the universe and guides the Jewish nation to its ultimate destiny. Over the centuries Jews subscribed to these beliefs and remained loyal to the tradition. In line with these tenets, Jewry observed the 613 commandments in scripture, and followed the rabbinic ordinances based on these divine laws. This religious system offered a framework for Jewish life, and provided Jews with a source of inspiration as they were faced with hostility from the Gentile world.

As Chapter 2 illustrates, the Jews have been a separate people, dedicated to their religious heritage. As such, they were constantly despised by their neighbours. In the Greco-Roman world they were viewed as detestable parasites; with the rise of Christianity, Jews were depicted as Christ-killers. As time passed the fathers of the Church developed an *Adversos Judaeos* tradition which vilified the Jews. In the Middle Ages, Jewish communities were massacred by crusaders and accused of the most heinous crimes. Such antipathy forced Jewry to turn inward. Centuries of anti-Semitism compelled Jews to defend their faith, and paradoxically led to the revitalization of Jewish religious life.

Yet, understandably Jews were anxious to escape from discrimination and persecution and therefore welcomed the opportunities offered by Jewish emancipation in modern times. As Chapter 3 demonstrates, Gentile advocates of Jewish emancipation such as Wilhelm Christian Dohm created a climate favourable to Jewish liberation. At the end of the eighteenth century, various Jewish restrictions were abolished, and under Napoleon's influence Jews gained a measure of equality in Western Europe. By the end of the nineteenth century, Jews entered into the mainstream of western society.

As Chapter 4 shows, such changes led to a revolution in Jewish life. The Jewish Enlightenment was spearheaded by the eighteenth-century philosopher Moses Mendelssohn who encouraged his co-religionists to integrate into the societies in which they lived. The Jewish Enlightenment brought about major changes in Jewish life; no longer were Jews isolated from European currents of culture and thought. Anxious to reform the faith, a number of Jewish figures such as Israel Jacobson sought to modernize the Jewish religion. In their view, traditional Jewish beliefs and practices had become outdated; what was necessary, they believed, was to create a new form of Judaism for the modern age. In the absence of virulent Jew-hatred, these reformers outlined a programme of religious reform which was bitterly criticized by champions of Orthodoxy.

Initially Reform Judaism was preoccupied with liturgical change. However, later in the nineteenth century attempts were made radically to reconstruct the Jewish religion. As Chapter 5 explains, the principles of Reform were set out at a gathering of Reform rabbis in Pittsburgh, Pennsylvania in 1885. In contrast with traditional Jewish theology, the Pittsburgh Platform called for a radical revision of previous belief. The Bible was to be subjected to scientific research, and rabbinic ordinances were to be discarded if they ceased to have spiritual significance. Reformers rejected the doctrine of the Messiah as well as the rabbinic understanding of a future life. Both in

Europe and America, Reform Judaism called for a new vision of Judaism for contemporary life.

Given the new freedoms of the modern age, other forms of Judaism soon developed under the impact of the Enlightenment. As Chapter 6 points out, Conservative Judaism similarly provided Jews in the United States with a non-traditional interpretation of the Jewish faith. Although less radical than Reform Judaism, the Conservative movement nonetheless rejected the doctrine of *Torah MiSinai* (the belief that the written and oral law were revealed by God to Moses on Mount Sinai). Instead, as Chapter 6 demonstrates, Conservative thinkers were determined that modern Jews should adopt a scientific approach to the Jewish heritage in the quest to reformulate Jewish life for modern times. Here, too, the spirit of tolerance brought about a dramatic transformation of Judaism.

For some Jews, however, such reforms to the faith were not sufficiently dramatic. The twentieth-century Jewish theologian Mordecai Kaplan argued that Jews should abandon a belief in a supernatural deity. In his view, traditional Jewish theology is outmoded – in its place, he sought to reconstruct Judaism without supernaturalism. As Chapter 7 explains, Reconstructionist Judaism emerged under his influence, and has now become a major movement. Adopting a naturalistic understanding of the nature of the divine, Reconstructionists continue to observe various aspects of Jewish law.

Like Reconstructionists, Humanistic Jews have rejected traditional Jewish theism. As Chapter 8 shows, this new movement offers a non-theistic interpretation of the Jewish faith. Under the leadership of Rabbi Sherwin Wine, Humanistic Judaism has redefined Jewishness, and focuses on the humanistic values of the tradition. In *Judaism Beyond God*, Wine explains that modern Jews must divest themselves of the biblical and rabbinic understanding of God in their quest to live religiously as Jews in the modern age.

The emergence of these non-Orthodox movements demonstrates the lack of religious coherence in the Jewish community. Under conditions of tolerance and freedom, the vast majority of Jews have distanced themselves from the traditional Jewish way of life. Many have totally assimilated and divorced themselves entirely from Judaism. As Chapter 9 illustrates, these assimilated Jews have deliberately separated themselves from the Jewish community. Some simply live a secular lifestyle with no connection to the Jewish establishment; others have intermarried. Some have even converted to other faiths. In all cases, they have deliberately rejected any institutional form of Judaism.

This survey of modern Judaism illustrates the disintegration of the traditional Jewish way of life in contemporary society. Without the constraints imposed by Jew-hatred, modern Jews have consciously rejected their religious heritage. As Chapter 10 shows, this has been the result of Enlightenment values. Under the impact of modern science and contemporary secular trends, the monolithic system of Jewish belief and practice has dissolved. In the past, anti-Semitism paradoxically compelled Jews to turn inwards. As a consequence, the tradition survived. However, as Jews gained civil and social acceptance, they largely discarded their religious heritage. It is thus a paradox of Jewish history that anti-Semitism and Jewish survival are intrinsically interconnected.

Part II continues this discussion with an account of the ways in which Jewish life was renewed in the past. As we noted, throughout history the Jewish people have been subject to discrimination, persecution and murder. Yet, despite this tragic history Jews have found strength under oppression. Determinedly they resisted their enemies. Through three millennia of suffering, they remained loyal to God and the covenant. Jew-hatred has thus played a central role in encouraging Jews to regenerate Jewish life through the study of the tradition and the observance of God's commandments.

Chapter 11 begins with the biblical account of the suffering of the ancient Israelites under Egyptian rule. According to the Hebrew scriptures, the Jewish people were enslaved, but with God's assistance they were able to overcome their enemies. This act of deliverance is celebrated during the festival of Passover. As a central orienting event in the life of the nation, it symbolizes God's providential care. The *Haggadah* is pervaded by the image of God as deliverer and saviour, and the story of the exodus teaches that God is on the side of the oppressed. In the face of hostility and contempt, the Jews are able to triumph against those who seek to destroy the Jewish people.

This survey continues in Chapter 12 with a discussion of the history of oppression and persecution. Once the Jewish people settled in the land of Canaan, they were besieged by their enemies, and eventually the Northern Kingdom was destroyed by the Assyrians. In the sixth century BCE, the Babylonian conquest devastated the Southern Kingdom. Bemoaning their fate, the exiles in Babylonia lamented the loss of their homeland. Yet, here again, the message of scripture is one of hope. The post-exilic prophets foretold the return of the Jewish people to their ancient homeland. Reassuring the nation, they prophesied that the Lord would return in triumph to Jerusalem. The theme of victory over despair is also a central message of the festival of *Purim* which commemorates the victory of the Jewish people during the Second Temple period. In a similar vein, the festival of *Hanukkah* celebrates the triumph of the Jewish nation over the Seleucids who had polluted the temple in the second century BCE.

As Chapter 13 explains, the destruction of the temple by the Romans in the first century CE led to the rebirth of the nation. Despite the devastating Roman onslaught, the Jewish religion was sustained by the Pharisees who established academies in Judea where the law was studied and expanded. Under the leadership of such figures as Hillel and Shammai, these sages continued the traditions of their forefathers. This reorientation of Jewish life brought about a regeneration of Judaism in the Holy Land and beyond. By the fourth century Jewish scholars had collected together the teachings of generations of rabbis: these extended discussions became the Palestinian *Talmud*. In Babylonia, scholarly activity also flourished, and by the sixth century Babylonian sages completed the redaction of the Babylonian *Talmud*. These developments were the direct result of the Roman onslaught against Judaism and the Jewish nation.

With the rise of Christianity, the Jewish community was subject to increased hostility. As Chapter 14 demonstrates, Jew-hatred was fostered by Church leaders who developed an *Adversos Judaeos* tradition. In treatises, discourses and sermons, the Church fathers castigated Jewry for refusing to accept Christ. According to these scholars, the Jewish people were the enemies of God. This early Christian onslaught on Judaism and the Jewish community had a deep impact on Jewish life. Detested by the Christian world, Jews turned inward and developed their own separate way of life divorced from the societies in which they lived. Jewish study took place in important centres of the Jewish world, producing distinguished rabbinic sages. During this period the study of the *Talmud* reached new heights. Similarly, drawing on the works of earlier thinkers, Jewish philosophers defended the faith from attack. These developments illustrate the vibrancy of Judaism despite the destructive impact of Christian antipathy to the Jewish faith.

Chapter 15 continues the history of Christian anti-Semitism. The traditions of the early Church fathers continued throughout the Middle Ages. During this period Jews were accused of the most heinous crimes: murdering Christian children to incorporate their blood in the preparation of unleavened bread at Passover; profaning the host; and practising sorcery against the Christian community. Throughout the Middle Ages, the Jewish community was detested, and stereotypes of the demonic Jew pervaded Christian literature. Yet, despite such opposition, the Jews united in defending their traditions. Alongside rabbinic scholarship and philosophical exploration, Jewish mystics produced sublime works of mystical reflection including the *Zohar*. Christian contempt for Jewry thus did not overwhelm the community. Instead, Jewish life flourished in the face of contempt and hostility. Even in the most terrible circumstances, they turned to God confident that he would deliver them from their oppressors.

By the end of the fourteenth century, Jews came to be regarded with suspicion and hostility. A large number of Jews were forcibly converted. These converts (*conversos*) outwardly lived as Christians, but secretly observed various aspects of the Jewish faith. Determined to root out these heretics, the Church embarked on an official inquisition. As Chapter 16 makes clear, the inquisitors used torture to exact confessions, and thousands were burned at the stake. In response, the *conversos* were haunted by a sense of self-reproach for their act of apostasy, and their prayers express a strong sense of remorse. Some sought to de-Christianize themselves by following bizarre practices. Others sought to escape the Spanish Inquisition by seeking refuge in other lands. There they were able to return to the traditions of their ancestors without fear of persecution. This tragic chapter of Jewish history thus reveals the Jewish determination to uphold the Jewish heritage under the most oppressive conditions.

As Chapter 17 relates, hostility toward Judaism continued into the early modern period. In the middle of the seventeenth century, a terrible attack against the Polish Jewish community was unleashed by the Cossacks. Jews were murdered in the most horrific fashion in this onslaught. Yet the faithful viewed this tragedy as the birth pangs of the Messiah, and during this period of persecution, Jewish hopes for deliverance were raised by the appearance of a self-proclaimed Messiah, Shabbatai Zevi. Throughout the Jewish world Jews believed they were living in the final days of redemption. In time Shabbatai was brought before the Sultan and given the choice between conversion to Islam or death. When he chose to convert, his followers were devastated. These events, however, did not undermine Jewish hope for the future. As the belief in the Messiah receded in importance, Jews championed the cause of emancipation from the tyranny of the past. The clarion call for liberty, equality and fraternity signified the dawning of a new age. In addition, Zionists envisaged the creation of a Jewish homeland in Palestine as the salvation of the Jewish people. Out of tragedy and despair, Jews longed for a better world.

Chapter 18 recounts the fulfilment of these longings for a place of refuge. Modern secular Zionism was grounded in the writings of Moses Hess, Leon Pinsker and Theodor Herzl who argued that Jews will never be secure in the countries where they live. Throughout history Jews have been accused of crucifying Jesus, drinking the blood of Christians, poisoning wells, exacting usury and despoiling their neighbours. In the view of these writers, Judaism and anti-Semitism are inseparably linked. The only solution to the Jewish problem is for Jews to have their own country. Old prejudices against Jewry are ingrained in society, and cannot be removed. At the end of the nineteenth century Zionists met together, and in a series of congresses they struggled to bring to fruition the vision of a Jewish state. The creation of a Jewish homeland was thus the direct result of anti-Semitic attitudes through the centuries.

In the quest to create a Jewish homeland in Palestine, Jewish settlers were compelled to struggle against the indigenous Arab population who were bitter opponents of Zionist aspirations. As Chapter 19 explains, in the 1920s Arab mobs attacked Jews in the Old City. This uprising was promoted by the Grand Mufti who attempted to provoke Jew-hatred. In the 1930s a popular national movement was founded which brought the cause of the Palestinians to the forefront of Pan-Arab concerns. During this period the Grand Mufti joined forces with the Nazis against the Jews. Such hostility, however, did not quell Jewish determination to create a Jewish state. Jewish pioneers were determined to overcome Arab opposition as well as the harsh conditions of the country. Again as in previous centuries, Jews were determined to triumph against their enemies.

The final chapter explores the resilience of the faithful under Nazi rule. As a racial state the Third Reich excluded Jews from participation in German life. Later, during the Holocaust Jews from both Western and Eastern Europe were transported to death camps where millions were murdered. Although many were traumatized by their experiences in the ghettos of Eastern Europe and in the camps, others went to their deaths believing in God's mercy. Paradoxically this onslaught against the Jewish people – as in other examples we have surveyed – evoked a deeply religious response. Many desired to live and die as their religious way of life demanded. There were numerous examples of religious heroism in the face of suffering and horror.

These examples demonstrate the ways in which Jewish tragedy has given rise to hope. In the face of oppression, persecution and murder, Jews remained faithful to the Jewish heritage and sought to renew Jewish life. This was the case in biblical times, and it has remained so through the centuries. Jew-hatred has thus had a paradoxical effect on Jewish consciousness. Rather than being overwhelmed by the forces against them, Jews have consistently sought to renew the Jewish faith. Anti-Semitism and Jewish renewal are therefore interlinked. Jew-hatred is, of course, to be deplored. Jews should make every effort to eliminate all forms of hostility to the Jewish nation. Yet at the same time, we should recognize that hatred of Jews and Judaism has led to the revitalization of the Jewish heritage. This is a salutary lesson in the modern world where the traditional Jewish way of life appears to be disappearing as Jews have gained social, civil and religious acceptance.

PART I

THE ENLIGHTENMENT AND THE DISINTEGRATION OF THE JEWISH WAY OF LIFE

Traditional Judaism

Until the period of the Enlightenment, Jews were united by a common tradition. The origins of traditional Judaism stretch back across 4,000 years to the beginning of the Jewish nation. From the patriarchal period to the institution of rabbinic Judaism in the Hellenistic period, Jews were bound by the covenant contracted with Moses on Mount Sinai. Through later centuries Jews continued to observe divine commandments in obedience to God's decree. Despite constant attack from Jew-haters, the Jewish community remained loyal to their ancient heritage.

The Orthodox Way of Life

The term 'Orthodox' is a relatively new invention; it was used during the Enlightenment in the nineteenth century to refer to Judaism as it was practised through the centuries. For traditionalists, any alteration to this ancient, evolving tradition was viewed as heresy. Reformers were condemned for corrupting the faith. Traditionalists championed the old ways (which they called 'Orthodox Judaism') in opposition to modernists who sought to revolutionize Jewish existence. In my Introduction to Judaism course, I normally begin with an outline of the development of Judaism from ancient times to the present. In explaining the nature of traditional Judaism, I emphasize that various groupings emerged in the history of the nation: Pharisees, Sadducees, Essenes, Karaites, Hasidim and Mitnaggedim. Nonetheless, there has been a common core of religious doctrine and observance.

As far as belief is concerned, the twelfth-century philosopher Moses Maimonides formulated in his *Commentary to the Mishnah* what he viewed as the central principles of the faith. This series of dogmas (which has been universally embraced by the Orthodox world) appears in the traditional prayerbook:

1. I believe with perfect faith that the Creator, blessed be his Name, is the Author and Guide of everything that has been created, and that he alone has made, does make, and will make all things.

2. I believe with perfect faith that the Creator, blessed be his Name, is a Unity, and that there is no unity in any manner like unto his, and that he alone is our God, who was, is, and will be.

3. I believe with perfect faith that the Creator, blessed be his Name, is not a body, and that he is free from all the properties of matter, and that he has not any form whatsoever.

4. I believe with perfect faith that the Creator, blessed be his Name, is the first and the last.

5. I believe with perfect faith that to the Creator, blessed be his Name, and to him alone, it is right to pray, and that it is not right to pray to any being besides him.

6. I believe with perfect faith that all the words of the prophets are true.

7. I believe with perfect faith that the prophecy of Moses our teacher, peace be unto him, was true, and that he was the chief of the prophets, both of those that preceded and of those that followed.

8. I believe with perfect faith that the whole *Torah*, now in our possession, is the same that was given to Moses our teacher, peace be unto him.

9. I believe with perfect faith that this *Torah* will not be changed, and that there will never be any other Law from the Creator, blessed be his Name.

10. I believe with perfect faith that the Creator, blessed be his Name, knows every deed of the children of men, and all their thoughts, as it is said, It is he that fashioneth the hearts of them all, that giveth heed to all their works.

11. I believe with perfect faith that the Creator, blessed be his Name, rewards those that keep his commandments, and punishes those that transgress them.

12. I believe with perfect faith in the coming of the Messiah; and, though he tarry, I will wait daily for his coming.

13. I believe with perfect faith that there will be a revival of the dead at the time when it shall please the Creator, blessed be his Name, and exalted be his fame for ever and ever.[1]

Although Orthodox Judaism is a religion of law, religious belief serves as the foundation of the tradition. According to Maimonides, these beliefs are of fundamental importance. Anyone who forsakes any of them forfeits his right to enter into the World-to-Come. 'When all these principles are in the safe keeping of man,' he wrote, 'and his conviction of them is well established, he then enters "into the general body of Israel", and it is incumbent upon us to love him, to care for him, and to do for him all that God commanded us to do for one another in the way of affection and brotherly sympathy.'[2]

But he warned:

> When ... a man breaks away from any of these funda-
> mental principles of belief, then of him it is said that
> 'he has gone out of the general body of Israel', and
> 'he denies the root truth of Judaism.' And he is then
> termed 'heretic' (*min*) and 'unbeliever' (*epiqoros*) ...
> and it is obligatory upon us to hate him and cause
> him to perish.[3]

This then is the foundation of the faith. Through the centuries, Jews have subscribed to these beliefs and remained loyal to the tradition. In line with these central tenets, rabbinic sages through the ages conceived of God as a divine unity who is transcendent, imminent, eternal, omnipotent, omniscient and all-good. In traditional Judaism, such a conviction serves as the basis for Jewish existence.

Where is such belief expressed? The Hebrew Bible serves as the starting point: here the Israelites experienced God as the Lord of history. The most uncompromising expression of his unity is the *Shema* prayer: 'Hear O Israel, the Lord our God, is one Lord' (Deut. 6:4). According to scripture, the universe owes its existence to one God, the creator of heaven and earth.

For the Jew, God has neither beginning nor end. In the Bible, the term *olam* is most frequently used to denote the concept of God's eternity. This biblical teaching was later elaborated by rabbinic sages who maintained that God was, is and for ever will be. Hence, in Maimonides' formulation of the 13 principles of Judaism, the belief that God is eternal is the fourth tenet. 'This means', he wrote, 'that the unity whom we have described is first in the absolute sense. No existent thing outside him is primary in relation to him.'[4]

The one eternal creator not only transcends the cosmos, he is conceived within traditional Judaism as imminent. Throughout history believers affirmed that God acts in the world, guiding it to its ultimate destiny. In ancient times the psalmist proclaimed what has become a central conviction of the faithful:

Whither shall I go from Thy spirit?
Or whither shall I flee from Thy presence?
If I ascend to heaven, Thou art there!
If I make my bed in *Sheol*, Thou art there!
If I take the wings of the morning
and dwell in the uttermost parts of the sea,
even there thy hand shall lead me. (Ps. 139:7–12)

From biblical times to the present, the belief in God's omnipotence has also been a major feature of traditional Judaism. Although the rabbis debated whether God can do everything, they universally affirmed that he is almighty in power. Similarly, Orthodox Judaism asserts that God's knowledge is not limited by space and time. Nothing is hidden from his sight. In the Bible the psalmist declared:

> The Lord looks down from heaven,
> He sees all the sons of men ...
> He who fashions the hearts of them all,
> and observes all their deeds. (Ps. 33:13, 15)

Again in Psalm 139 we read:

> Thou knowest when I sit down and when I rise up;
> Thou discernest my thoughts from afar.
> Thou searchest out my path and my lying down,
> and art acquainted with all my ways. (Ps. 139:2–3)

In the past Jewish thinkers wrestled with the question how human beings could have free will given such a conception of omniscience and providence. Nevertheless, Orthodox Judaism maintains that there is no contradiction between these seemingly incompatible beliefs. Maimonides, for example, stated in his *Guide for the Perplexed* that God knows all things before they occur. Nonetheless, human beings are unable to comprehend the nature of God's knowledge because it is of a different order from that of human beings. On this account it is similarly not possible to understand how divine foreknowledge is compatible with human freedom.

Further, Jewish sages maintained that expositions and elaborations of the written law in the Five Books of Moses were also revealed by God to Moses on Mount Sinai. Subsequently they were passed from generation to generation and through this process additional legislation was incorporated. This process is referred to as the oral *Torah*. Thus traditional Judaism affirms that God's revelation is twofold and binding for all time. Committed to this belief, Orthodox Jews pray in the synagogue that God will guide them to do his will. Orthodoxy is thus committed to the view that the written and oral *Torah* were imparted by God to Moses on Mount Sinai.

The legal system of the *Torah* serves as the background for the understanding of sin and atonement in traditional Judaism. In the Bible sin is seen as a transgression against God's law. A sinner is one who has not fulfilled his obligations to God. According to rabbinic Judaism, sins can be classified in terms of their gravity as indicated by the punishments prescribed by biblical law. Orthodox Judaism further teaches that there are two tendencies in every person: the good inclination (*yetzer ha-tov*) and the evil inclination (*yetzer ha-ra*). As far as atonement for sin is concerned, traditional Judaism teaches that it can be attained after a process of repentance involving the recognition of sin.

For Orthodox Jews, the election of Israel as God's chosen people is central to the understanding of law. Through its election Israel was given a historic mission to bear divine truth to humanity. Divine election demands reciprocal response. Israel is obligated to keep God's statutes and observe his laws. Traditional Judaism views

God's covenant with his people as enshrined in law as the foundation of the faith. Yet Orthodox Judaism is also preoccupied with eternal deliverance and salvation.

According to the sages, the World-to-Come is divided into several stages. First there is the time of messianic redemption. On the basis of biblical prophecy, the rabbis believed that the prophet Elijah would return prior to the coming of the Messiah to resolve all earthly problems. The *Talmud* declares that the messianic age is to take place on earth after a period of decline and calamity and will result in the fulfilment of every human wish. Peace will reign throughout nature; Jerusalem will be rebuilt; and at the close of this era, the dead will be resurrected and rejoined with their souls and a final judgement will come upon all humanity.

These then are the central beliefs of the faith. Orthodox Judaism, however, is not defined solely by belief: in addition, religious observance is paramount. Through the centuries Jews have maintained that God revealed 613 commandments to Moses on Mount Sinai. These *mitzvot* are recorded in the Five Books of Moses; they consist of:

1. Statutes concerned with ritual performances characterized as obligations between human beings and God.
2. Judgements consisting of ritual laws that would have been adopted by society even if they had not been decreed by God.

These 613 commandments consist of 365 negative and 248 positive prescriptions.

Traditional Judaism maintains that Moses received the oral *Torah* in addition to the written law. This chain of tradition was passed down from generation to generation, as the *Mishnah* declares:

> Moses received the *Torah* on Mount Sinai and passed it on to Joshua and Joshua to the elders, and the elders to the prophets, and the prophets to the men of the Great Assembly ... Simon the righteous was one of the last members of the Great Assembly ... Antigonus of Socho received the *Torah* from Simon the Righteous ... Yose ben Yoezer of Zeredah and Yose ben Yohanan of Jerusalem received the *Torah* from them ... Joshua ben Perahyah and Nittai the Arbelite received the *Torah* from them ... Judah ben Tabbai and Simeon ben Shetah received the *Torah* from them ... Shemayah and Avtalyon received the *Torah* from them ... Hillel and Shammai received the *Torah* from them ... Rabban Johanan ben Zakkai received the *Torah* from Hillel and Shammai.[5]

In subsequent generations sages continued to discuss the content of Jewish law: their deliberations are recorded in the Palestinian and Babylonian *Talmuds* which are arranged according to the structure of the *Mishnah*. Both *Talmuds* incorporate the *Mishnah* and later rabbinic discussions known as the *Gemara*. The *Gemara* text preserves the proceedings of the academies in both Palestine and Babylonia, where scholars assembled to study the *Mishnah*. The central purpose of these deliberations was to elucidate the *Mishnah* text.

After the compilation of the *Talmuds* in the sixth century CE, scholars continued the development of Jewish law by issuing answers to specific questions. These responses touched on all aspects of Jewish law and ensured a standardization of practice. In time various scholars felt the need to produce codes of Jewish law so that all members of the community would have access to the legal tradition. In the eleventh century Isaac Alfasi produced a work that became the standard code for Sephardic Jewry. Two centuries later, Asher ben Jehiel wrote a code that became the code for Ashkenazi Jews. Moses Maimonides in the twelfth century also wrote an important code that had a wide influence, as did the code by Jacob ben Asher in the fourteenth century.

In the sixteenth century Joseph Caro published the *Shulkhan Arukh*, which together with glosses by Moses Isserles has served as the standard *Code of Jewish Law* for Orthodox Jewry until the present day. This extensive work covers all aspects of Jewish life, and is viewed as the framework for authentic Jewish existence. These few examples are typical of its numerous legal prescriptions:

1. It is written (Micah 6:8): 'And to walk humbly with thy God.' Therefore it is the duty of every man to be modest in all his ways. When putting on or removing his shirt or any other undergarment, he should be careful not to expose his body unduly. He should put it on or remove it while still lying in bed. He should never say to himself: 'Lo, I am all alone in my inner chamber and in the dark, who can see me?'

2. A person should accustom himself to respond to the call of nature once in the evening and once in the morning; such a habit is conducive to alertness and cleanliness. If he is unable to ease himself, he should walk a distance of four cubits, repeating it several times if need be; or he should divert attention from other matters.

3. A man must exercise modesty when in the lavatory; he should not expose himself before he sits down, and should not expose his body more than is actually necessary.

4. When in the lavatory, it is forbidden to think of sacred matters; it is therefore best to concentrate there upon one's business affairs and accounts so that one may not be led to think either of holy matters or, God forbid, indulge in sinful thoughts.

5. After each defecation or urination, even of one drop, one must wash one's hands and say the benediction '*Asher yatzar*'. If one has forgotten to say the benediction, and after having responded to the call of nature again, one became aware of one's neglect, one need not say the benediction more than once.[6]

In the modern Jewish world, ultra-Orthodox Jews remain committed to the traditional Jewish way of life. Determined to keep the covenant, their lives are circumscribed by the laws passed down from generation to generation. Out of love and awe, they worship the God whom they believe freed their ancestors from bondage and guides the destiny of his chosen people. Such observance is not perceived as a burden, but as a source of joy and fulfilment. Although these individuals constitute only a small segment of the Jewish community, they are devoted to the tradition. A strictly Orthodox Jew whom my wife and I interviewed for our book *The American Jew* explained such dedication:

> Judaism smacks in the face of a lot of the philosophies and ways and beliefs of American society. To that I say: 'If Abraham had caved in to the beliefs of his time, we would all now be pagans. Judaism did not give in to the times ... that's how it remained Judaism! ... There's a very beautiful song and when I got married I marched down to the marriage canopy to its tune: 'Behold the days are coming, promises God, and I will send a hunger in the land, not a hunger for bread, not a thirst for water, but to hear the word of God.'[7]

Here then is the traditional framework for Jewish living which is grounded in sacred sources. For nearly four millennia Jews have been united in their belief that they are God's chosen people. Recipients of the revelation to Moses on Mount Sinai, they remained faithful to the covenant, convinced that they would receive their ultimate reward in the World-to-Come. When faced by their enemies, they turned to God for support. Courageously, they faced a hostile world, animated by faith in the God of Abraham, Isaac and Jacob who would not forsake them in their time of need.

The Threat of Anti-Semitism

From ancient times, Jews have been a separate people, dedicated to their religious traditions. As we have seen, traditional Judaism consists of a system of belief and practice grounded in the conviction that God chose the Jews as his special people and guides their ultimate destiny. Yet, through the centuries Jews have suffered for their faith – repeatedly they were assailed by their enemies. Nonetheless, despite such attacks, they were determined to remain loyal to their sacred heritage.

The History of Anti-Semitism

Typical of the diatribes levelled at Jewry through the centuries was Martin Luther's attack on Judaism and the Jewish nation published in 1542. In *Against the Jews and Their Lies*, he depicted the Jewish nation as an unwanted pestilence:

> Nobody wants them. The countryside and the roads are open to them: they may return to their country when they wish; we shall gladly give them presents to get rid of them, for they are a heavy burden on

us, a scourge, a pestilence and misfortune for our country.[1]

What is to be done with this foreign element? Luther proposed a number of remedies:

> First, their synagogues should be set on fire, and whatever does not burn up should be covered or spread with dirt so that no one may ever be able to see a cinder of stone of it. And this ought to be done for the honour of God and of Christianity in order that God may see that we are Christians, and that we have not wittingly tolerated or approved of such public lying, cursing and blaspheming of his son and his Christians ... Secondly, their homes should likewise be broken down and destroyed. For they perpetuate the same things there that they do in their synagogues ... Thirdly, they should be deprived of their prayer-books and *Talmuds* in which such idolatry, lies, cursing and blasphemy are taught. Fourthly, their rabbis must be forbidden under threat of death to teach any more.[2]

For Martin Luther, the Jews were detestable aliens, members of a race who had denied Christ. Such hostility to Jewry had a long legacy, stretching back to the earliest history of the Church. With the emergence of Christianity, the followers of Christ believed themselves to be the true heirs of the covenant. For these Christians Jesus' messiahship was understood as bringing about a new age in which the true Israel will become a light to the nations. Given this eschatological vision, the Jewish people were regarded with animosity. The writers of the Gospels depicted Jesus attacking the leaders of the nation, and the church taught that circumcision of the heart – rather than obedience to the law – was what God required.

In proclaiming this message, Paul stressed that the Jewish nation had been rejected by God and that the old covenant had been superseded. For Paul, those who belong to the Mosaic covenant will be cast out, but the children of the new covenant will be saved in Christ. Paul's diatribe against the Jews is a rejection of the Jewish tradition: the Mosaic covenant belongs to an apostate people. Yet, God's true covenant was given before the revelation on Mount Sinai and will be fulfilled with the advent of the messianic age. Only those who belong to this spiritual community will be vouchsafed the divine promises contained in scripture.

In the fourth Gospel the repudiation of Judaism is conceived as an antithesis between a fulfilled spiritual universe of Christ and a fallen world of darkness represented by the Jewish people. Jesus is the spiritual temple in contrast to the Jewish temple which will be destroyed. Jesus is the spiritual water of eternal life, rather than the physical water of Jacob's well. Jesus is the bread of truth as opposed to the manna of the wilderness that did not last. Only those who know Christ can know God, and apart from the knowledge of Christ there is no knowledge of God: 'I am the way, and the truth, and the life: no one comes to the Father but by me' (John 14:6).

In light of this teaching the fathers of the church developed an *Adversos Judaeos* tradition which vilified the

Jews. According to the Church fathers, Jews were guilty in the past of indecent actions and they have continued to be a contemptible people. Given such behaviour, God's promises in the future apply only to the Church. Basing their views on scripture, the Church fathers argued that the struggle between Judaism and Christianity was prefigured in the Bible. By rejecting Christ, Jews have been rejected and are doomed for eternity. Christians, rather than the Jewish nation, thus constitute God's elect. As the religion of the Roman empire, Christianity was to serve as an instrument for spreading the promise of God's redemption to humanity.

The tradition of Christian anti-Semitism as created by the Church fathers continued through the centuries. In the fourth and fifth centuries a series of legislative measures were taken by both the church and the empire – these laws were a concrete reflection of patristic teaching about the Jews. At the beginning of the century the Council of Elvira in Spain forbade intermarriage between Jews and Christians except where the Jewish partner had converted to Christianity. The Council of Antioch (341) prohibited Christians from celebrating Passover with Jews. The Council of Laodicea (434–81) forbade Christians from keeping the Jewish sabbath or from receiving gifts of unleavened bread from Jews.

These edicts were followed by the *Codex Theodosianus*, a compilation of law issued from the time of Constantine, which was promulgated in 438. Although this codex does guarantee certain rights to the Jewish population, it bans conversion to Judaism as well as the circumcision of slaves of Jewish owners. In addition, the codex bars

Jews from public functions, administrative posts and the legal profession. Marriages to Jews were also prohibited. Throughout this codex there are numerous insulting references to the Jewish faith – Judaism is referred to as a wicked sect, and Jews are described as abominable. The *Justinian Code* issued in 529 also denied Jews various rights.

Later, during the crusades, Jewish communities were decimated throughout Western Europe. Such hostility towards Jews was intensified by various charges levelled against the Jewish population. Frequently Jews were accused of killing Christian children to use their blood in preparations for the Passover. Jews were also charged with blaspheming the Christian faith in the *Talmud* – as a result, this sacred text was cast to the flames. Further, Jews were blamed for causing the Black Plague by poisoning wells. Yet despite this onslaught on the Jewish community, many Jewish martyrs went to their deaths, confident that their tormentors would be punished eternally for their sins.

Throughout the Middle Ages, the Jew was represented as a dark, demonic figure; repeatedly Jews were accused of possessing the attributes of both the devil and witches. As the personification of evil, they were regarded as sub-human. In addition, Jews were viewed as magicians, able to work magic against neighbouring Christians. On this basis, the Jewish population was accused of desecrating the host for magical purposes and committing acts of ritual murder. Repeatedly they were charged with murdering Christian children to incorporate their blood into unleavened bread for

Passover. Such allegations of ritual murder spread from country to country, and many Jews were victimized for supposedly committing such atrocious acts.

Although the Jewish community was expelled from France in the fourteenth century, negative images of Jews continued to play a role in French culture. Catechisms, lives of Jesus, and canticles portrayed the Jewish people as tools of Satan. In the lives of Jesus and the saints, as well as in the accounts of pilgrimages, the Jewish population was presented in the most horrific fashion. Thus in a fifteenth-century life of Jesus, his suffering is portrayed as the result of Jewish animosity:

> Some insulted him; others, with the backs of their hands, struck his noble and gentle mouth; others spit into his face; others tore out his beard or pulled at his hair, and thus trampled under their accursed feet the Lord of the angels ... And still spitting into his noble countenance, they struck his head with a stick, so that the thorns of his crown sank into his forehead.[3]

During this period tracts abounded which denounced the Jews in terms reminiscent of the Middle Ages. In this typical French example, Jews were presented as detested and accursed villains:

> Demons escaped from hell,
> Race of the Jews, detestable men,
> More accursed than Lucifer
> And more wicked than all the devils.
> Cruel tigers, begone,

> Unworthy as you are to live among us.
> When you thirst so for blood
> You must fear the punishment
> With which the Holy Inquisition
> Will chastise your parricides.
> Untie the hands and feet
> Of a citizen put to the torture.
> Would you make of him
> The image of an *Ecce Homo*
> Subject to insult and outrage?[4]

What should be done with this accursed nation? One text proposes that they should be hung:

> Let them be seen, hands and feet
> Bound, those of their horde
> Following the footsteps closely
> Of him whom they laid low
> By a death all too cruel.
> Let them be seen on the scaffold
> With no favour, grace or pardon.[5]

In England Jews were similarly vilified even though the Jewish nation was expelled in 1290. German Jews were also detested – such hostility was most powerfully expressed in Martin Luther's *Against the Jews and Their Lies*. Such publications were followed by a wide range of tracts which denigrated Judaism and the Jewish people. In fifteenth-century Spain the church initiated a new form of persecution. Under Ferdinand and Isabella the Inquisition was established to purge *conversos* or New

Christians – Jewish converts to Christianity as opposed to Old Christians of pure blood – who were suspected of practising Jewish customs. Tribunals were established throughout Spain which applied torture to extract confessions from the guilty – those who refused to confess were cast to the flames. Finally, at the end of the century, an Edict of Expulsion was enacted to rid the country of the Jewish race who had polluted the Christian population.

Unlike their co-religionists in Western Europe, Jews in Poland enjoyed considerable tolerance and were granted numerous privileges – they were not confined to ghettos, nor restricted in their occupations. Yet despite such prosperity, the country was subject to Christian anti-Jewish hostility in the late medieval period, and in the seventeenth century Polish Jewry was massacred by Cossacks under Bogdan Chmielnicki. According to contemporary accounts, Jews suffered in the most merciless fashion in this onslaught.

In the wake of this catastrophe, the Jewish community went into mourning. In 1650 the Council of the Four Nations proclaimed a national mourning in memory of the victims. New elegies were written and recited in synagogues following those that traditionally commemorate Jewish suffering during the crusades.

In Russia, antipathy towards Jewry was widespread. When, for example, Ivan the Terrible was urged by the Polish King Sigismund Augustus to allow several Jewish merchants into Moscow, he asserted:

> Apropos of what you write to persuade us to allow
> your Jews to enter our lands, we have already written

you several times, telling you of the vile actions of
the Jews, who have turned our people away from
Christ, introduced poisonous drugs into our state,
and caused much harm to our people. You should
be ashamed, our brother, to write us about them
knowing their misdeeds all the while. In other states
they have been expelled or put to death. We cannot
permit the Jews to come into our state, for we do not
wish to see any evil here.[6]

During the early modern period the commercial interests
of the bourgeoisie, coupled with centuries-old Christian
prejudice against Jews and Judaism, evoked considerable hostility towards the Jewish population in western
countries. In Germany, merchants protested against the
infidels living in their midst. Jewish trade, they believed,
would destroy the economic life of the country and
pollute the Christian population. Similar attitudes were
expressed in France, where the bourgeoisie resisted Jewish
settlement despite the fact that the nobility regarded Jews
as financially useful. In Great Britain, Jews were also
subject to virulent criticism, and attempts to simplify
procedures for Jewish naturalization and to authorize Jews
to possess land were met with considerable resistance.

Throughout the centuries, Jews were continually
stereotyped – repeatedly the allegation was made that
they exuded a particular smell in contrast to the Christian
odour of sanctity. In response to such distortion and
antipathy, the Jewish community turned inward,
despising those who denigrated them. In the intimacy
of the Jewish community, Jews mistrusted the Christian

world, rejected its values, and were indifferent to its views. Believing in their own moral superiority, they held firmly to the conviction that God had chosen them as his people. Devoted to the covenant, they adhered to ancient laws and customs of the Jewish tradition.

JEWISH EMANCIPATION
AND FREEDOM

Despite the hostility directed at Jewry through the centuries, the Jewish nation continued to remain loyal to the Jewish heritage. In the face of continued assault, they were convinced that God would ultimately redeem them and that the righteous of Israel would be rewarded in a future life. Notwithstanding such determination, Jews were anxious to escape from discrimination and persecution. Freed from the constraints of ghetto life, they were convinced that they could integrate into the societies in which they lived and thereby divest themselves of their former disabilities.

JEWISH EMANCIPATION

In the wake of the Enlightenment, the emancipation of Jews began to take place at the end of the eighteenth century. From Western Europe to the Russian empire humanist ideals began to stir the consciousness of the Christian population. By the 1770s and 1780s the treatment of Jews in Central Europe was greatly improved due to the influence of such polemicists as Wilhelm

Christian Dohm. In an influential tract, 'Concerning the Amelioration of the Civil Status of the Jews', Dohm argued that the Jews did not pose any threat and could become valuable and patriotic citizens. A wise and benevolent society, he stressed, should abolish restrictions which prevent the Jewish population from having close contact with Christians and acquiring secular knowledge. All occupations, he argued, should be open to Jews and educational opportunities should be provided.

In this tract, he wrote:

> Only common people believe that it is permissible to deceive a Jew or accuse him of being permitted by his law to deceive non-Jews. It is only bigoted clergy, who have collected tales of the prejudices of the Jews which are used to reinforce their own prejudices ... Jews have wisdom; they are intelligent and hard-working and dogged. They are capable of finding their own way in every situation ... If our arguments are correct, we shall find the oppression under which they suffer and the trade restrictions imposed on them are the real reason for their shortcomings. Therefore it follows that we have also discovered the means by which their faults may be cured and by which they will become both better human beings and more useful citizens.[1]

The holy Roman emperor Joseph II echoed such sentiments. In 1781 he abolished the Jewish badge as well as taxes imposed on Jewish travellers; in the following year he issued an edict of toleration which granted Jews of

Vienna freedom in trade and industry and the right of residence outside Jewish quarters. Moreover, regulations prohibiting Jews from leaving their homes before noon on Sunday and attending places of public amusement were abolished. Jews were also permitted to send their children to state schools or set up their own educational institutions:

> In order to make the Jews more useful, discriminatory Jewish clothing which has been worn in the past is now abolished. Within two years the Jews must abandon their own language; from now on all their contracts, bonds, wills, accounts, ledgers, certificates and any legally binding document must be drawn up in German ... Jews may continue to use their own language during religious services ... Jews who do not have the opportunity of sending their children to Jewish schools must send them to Christian ones to learn reading, writing, arithmetic and other subjects ... Jews will also be permitted to attend the imperial universities ... Leaders of local communities must rationally instruct their people that the Jews may be treated like any other fellow human being.[2]

As in Germany, reforms in France during the 1770s and 1780s improved the situation of the Jewish population. Though Sephardic Jews in Paris and in the south and southwest lived in comfort and security, the Ashkenazic Jews of Alsace and Lorraine had a traditional Jewish lifestyle and were subject to a variety of disabilities. In 1789 the National Assembly issued a declaration proclaiming that all human beings are born and remain free and equal in rights and that no person should be persecuted for his opinions as long as they do not subvert civil law. In 1790 the Sephardim of southwest France and Jews from Papal Avignon were granted citizenship. This decree was followed in September 1791 by a resolution which granted citizenship rights to all Jews. This change in Jewish status occurred elsewhere in Europe as well – in 1796 the Dutch Jews of the Batavian republic were also granted full citizenship rights and in 1797 the ghettos of Padua and Rome were abolished.

In 1799 Napoleon became the First Consul of France and five years later he was proclaimed emperor. Napoleon's *Code of Civil Law* propounded in 1804 established the right of all inhabitants to follow any trade and declared equality for all. After 1806 a number of German principalities were united in the French kingdom of Westphalia where Jews were granted the same rights. Despite these advances the situation of Jews did not undergo a complete transformation, and Napoleon still desired to regulate Jewish affairs. In July 1806 he convened an Assembly of Jewish Notables to consider a number of issues: Do Jewish marriage and divorce procedures conflict with French civil law? Are Jews allowed to marry Christians? Do French Jews consider Frenchmen their compatriots and is France their country?

In reply the Assembly decreed that Jewish law is compatible with French civil law; Jewish divorce and marriage are not binding unless preceded by a civil act; mixed marriage is legal but cannot be sanctioned by the Jewish faith; France is the homeland of the French Jews and Frenchmen should be seen as their kin. Convinced of their loyalty to France, the Assembly stated:

> Men who have adopted a country and who have lived there for many generations and who, even when certain of the country's laws have curtailed their civil rights, are so attached to it that they prefer the misfortune of civil disability to that of leaving, must be seen in France as Frenchmen. Jews regard the obligation of defending France as both an honourable and a precious duty. Jeremiah 29 strongly recommends the Jews to see Babylon as their country, even though they were only to stay there for seventy years. He tells them to cultivate the fields, to build houses, to sow and to plant. The Jews followed his advice to such an extent that, according to Ezra 2, when Cyrus allowed them to return to Jerusalem to rebuild the temple, only forty-two thousand, three hundred and sixty of them left Babylon. Mostly it was the poor people who went; the rich stayed in Babylon.

> Love of one's country is an entirely natural and lively sentiment among the Jews. It is completely in harmony with their religious beliefs that a French Jew in England feels himself to be a stranger, even in the company of English Jews. English Jews feel the same in France. Their patriotism is so great that in the last war French Jews could be found fighting against Jews of other countries with which France was at war. Many of them were honourably wounded and others

won on the field of battle fervent testimonies to their valour.[3]

In the next year Napoleon summoned a Grand *Sanhedrin* consisting of rabbis and laymen to confirm the views of the Assembly. This body pledged its allegiance to the emperor and nullified any features of Jewish tradition that conflicted with the particular requirements of citizenship. In 1808 Napoleon issued two edicts regarding the Jewish community. In the first he set up a system of district boards of rabbis and laymen (consistories) to regulate Jewish affairs under the supervision of a central body in Paris. These consistories were responsible for maintaining synagogues and religious institutions, enforcing laws of conscription, overseeing changes in occupations ordered by the government and acting as a local police force. Napoleon's second decree postponed, reduced or abrogated all debts owed to Jews, regulated Jewish trade and residence rights and prohibited Jewish army conscripts from hiring substitutes.

After Napoleon's defeat and abdication, the map of Europe was redrawn by the Congress of Vienna between 1814 and 1815, and in addition the diplomats at the Congress issued a resolution that instructed the German confederation to ameliorate the status of the Jews. Yet despite this decree the German governments disowned the rights of equality that had previously been granted to Jews by the French and instead imposed restrictions on residence and occupation. In place of the spirit of emancipation unleashed by the French Revolution, Germany became increasingly patriotic and xenophobic. Various academies maintained that the Jews were 'Asiatic aliens' and insisted that they could not enter into German-Christian culture without converting to Christianity.

In 1819 German Jewry was attacked in cities and the countryside during the Hep Hep Riots. In Berlin a contemporary account recorded:

> The excesses which have been committed against the Jews in several towns in Germany have given rise to fear amongst the Israelites in this capital. There have been some small scenes here already. A few of the Jews' enemies paid a fair number of ne'er-do-wells to cry Hep! Hep! under the windows of the country house of a banker of that nation. An old Israelite pedlar of ribbons and pencils was chased by delinquents in the street which echoed with the ominous cry; he made the best of it like a man with a sense of humour and continued on his way laughing and even shouting Hep! Hep! incessantly himself, but having taken it into his head to peer into a shop and shout inside, a woman who happened to be on the threshold dealt him a violent box on the ears, to which he immediately replied with another. A police employee, who was within call, took him under his protection and, to get him out of reach of the ill-treatment to which he was still exposed, conducted him to the police station.[4]

After 1830, however, a more liberal attitude prevailed and various writers advocated a more tolerant approach. The most important Jewish exponent of emancipation, Gabriel

Riesser, argued that the Jews were not a separate nation and were capable of loving Germany as their homeland. Jewish converts to Christianity such as Heinrich Heine also defended the rights of Jews during this period. Summing up the spirit of the period, he wrote:

> What is the great question of the age? It is Emancipation! Not just the emancipation of the Irish, the Greeks, the Jews of Frankfurt, the Negroes of the West Indies or of other oppressed groups, but the emancipation of the whole world ... which even now is pulling away from the leading strings of the aristocracy and the privileged classes.[5]

The French Revolution of 1848 which led to outbreaks in Prussia, Austria, Hungary, Italy and Bohemia forced rulers to grant constitutions which guaranteed freedom of speech, assembly and religion. In Germany a National Assembly was convened to draft a constitution which included a bill of rights designating civil, political and religious liberty for all Germans. Although this constitution did not come into effect because the Revolution was suppressed, the 1850s and 1860s witnessed economic and industrial expansion in Germany in which liberal politicians advocated a policy of civil equality. In 1869 the parliament of the North German Federation proclaimed Jewish emancipation for all its constituents, and in 1871, when all of Germany, excluding Austria, became the German Reich under the Hohenzollern dynasty, Jewish emancipation was complete. All restrictions concerning professions, marriage, real estate and the right to vote were eliminated.

Compared with the West, the social and political conditions of Eastern European Jewry were less conducive to emancipation. After the partitions of Poland in the latter half of the eighteenth century and the decision of the Congress of Vienna to place the Duchy of Warsaw under Alexander I, most of Polish Jewry were under Russian rule. At the beginning of the nineteenth century Russia preserved its previous social order: social classes were legally segregated; the aristocracy maintained its privileges; the peasantry lived as serfs; and the Church was under state control. In many towns and villages during this period Jews were in the majority and engaged in a wide range of occupations.

Initially Catherine the Great exhibited tolerance towards her Jewish subjects, but in 1791 Jewish merchants were prohibited from settling in Central Russia. In 1804 Alexander I specified territory in Western Russia as an area in which Jews would be allowed to reside, and this was known as the Pale of Settlement. After several attempts to expel Jews from the countryside, the Czar in 1817 initiated a new policy of integrating the Jewish community into the population by founding a Society of Israelite Christians which extended legal and financial concessions to baptized Jews. In 1824 the deportation of Jews from villages began; in the same year Alexander I died and was succeeded by Nicholas I who adopted a severe attitude to the Jewish community. In 1827 he initiated a policy of inducting Jewish boys into the Russian army for a 25-year period. Nicholas I also deported Jews from villages in certain areas.

In 1835 the Russian government propagated a revised code of laws to regulate Jewish settlement in the western border. In order to reduce Jewish isolation the government set out to reform education in 1841. Several years later Nicholas I abolished the *kehillot* and put Jewry under the authority of the police as well as municipal government. Despite this policy, it was impossible for the Russian administration to carry out the functions of the *kehillot*, and it was recognized that a Jewish body was needed to recruit students for state military schools and to collect taxes. Between 1850 and 1851 the government attempted to forbid Jewish dress, mens' sidecurls, and the ritual of shaving women's hair.

In 1851 a plan was initiated to categorize all Jews in the country along economic lines. Those who were considered useful subjects included craftsmen, farmers and wealthy merchants, whereas the vast majority of Jews were liable to further restrictions. After the Crimean War of 1853–6, Alexander II emancipated the serfs, modernized the judiciary and established a system of local self-government. In addition he allowed certain groups, including wealthy merchants, university graduates, certified artisans, discharged soldiers and all holders of diplomas to reside outside the Pale of Settlement. As a result Jewish communities appeared in St Petersburg and Moscow. Furthermore, a limited number of Jews were allowed to enter the legal profession and participate in district councils. Government-sponsored Jewish schools also attracted more Jewish students, and in the 1860s and

1870s emancipated Jews began to take an active role in the professions and in Russian economic life.

The Enlightenment thus provided a basis for the emancipation of Jewry. No longer were Jews insulated from non-Jewish currents of culture and thought, and this transformation heralded the beginning of a new age. As we have seen, in previous centuries Jews were despised because of their strange practices. From century to century, they were subject to repeated attack. However, with the encouragement of Christian polemicists such hostility began to lessen. Jews were no longer perceived as mysterious, demonic aliens; instead, they were encouraged to integrate into the countries in which they lived and contribute to the welfare of society.

4

THE JEWISH ENLIGHTENMENT
AND REFORM

In the wake of the Enlightenment, a number of Jewish thinkers, such as Moses Mendelssohn, sought to bring about a transformation of Jewish existence. Intent on encouraging his co-religionists to integrate into the surrounding culture, he translated the Pentateuch into German. In this way, he believed, Jews would be able to communicate with the non-Jewish world. His followers, the *maskilim*, similarly attempted to transcend the constrictions of ghetto life. In subsequent years, reformers championed the modernization of Judaism and the assimilation of Jews into western society.

MODERNIZING JUDAISM

The roots of Jewish thought during the Enlightenment go back to seventeenth-century Holland where a number of Jewish thinkers attempted to view the Jewish tradition in the light of the new scientific conception of the world. Uriel Acosta, for example, argued that the *Torah* was probably not of divine origin since it contained many features contrary to natural law. The greatest of these

Dutch Jewish thinkers was Baruch Spinoza who published a treatise, *Tractatus Theologico Politicus*, in which he rejected the medieval synthesis of faith and reason. In the first section of this work Spinoza maintained that the prophets possessed moral insight rather than theoretical truth. Rejecting the Maimonidean belief that the Bible contains a hidden esoteric meaning, Spinoza argued that the Hebrew scriptures were intended for the masses. As far as the *Torah* is concerned, it was not composed in its entirety by Moses – the historical books were compilations assembled by many generations.

For Spinoza the function of religion was to provide a framework for ethical action. Philosophy, on the other hand, is concerned with truth, and philosophers should be free to engage in philosophical speculation unconstrained by religious opinions. It is a usurpation of the social contract and a violation of human rights to legislate belief. On the basis of this view, Spinoza propounded a metaphysical system based on a pantheistic conception of nature.

Spinoza's rational reflections on theological matters provided the background to the philosophical enquiries of the greatest thinker of the Jewish Enlightenment, Moses Mendelssohn. Born in Dessau, Mendelssohn travelled to Berlin as a young student where he pursued secular as well as religious studies and befriended leading figures of the German Enlightenment such as Gotthold Ephraim Lessing. His one-act play *Die Jüden* was written in 1749 and published five years later; it is the earliest literary work by a European non-Jew to portray a Jew favourably. A later work, *Nathan der Weise*, depicts

Judaism, Christianity and Islam as three brothers. In this work, Nathan is a Jewish figure who preaches an enlightened approach based on common humanity.

Under Lessing's influence, Mendelssohn published a number of theological studies in which he argued for the existence of God and creation and propounded the view that human reason is able to discover the reality of God, divine providence and the immortality of the soul. When challenged by a Christian apologist to explain why he remained loyal to the Jewish faith, Mendelssohn published a defence of the Jewish religion, *Jerusalem*, in 1783. In this study Mendelssohn contended that no religious institution should use coercion; neither the Church nor the state, he believed, has the right to impose its religious views on the individual. Addressing the question as to whether the Mosaic law sanctions such coercion, Mendelssohn stressed that Judaism does not coerce the mind through dogma. Rather, he stated that the Israelites possess a divine legislation – laws, commandments, statutes, rules of conduct, instruction in God's will and in what they are to do to attain temporal and eternal salvation. In his view, Moses revealed to them these laws and commandments, but not dogmas.

The distinction Mendelssohn drew between natural religion and the Jewish faith was based on three types of truth. All human beings, he stated, have the innate capacity to discover the existence of God, providence and the hereafter. But Judaism is uniquely different from other religions in that it contains a revealed law. The Jewish people did not hear God proclaim that he is an eternal, necessary, omnipotent and omniscient being who rewards and punishes humankind. Instead divine commandments were revealed to God's chosen people. The purpose of this legal code was to make Israel into a priestly nation.

For Mendelssohn Jewish law does not give power to the authorities to persecute individuals for holding false doctrines. Yet Jews, he argued, should not absolve themselves from following God's law:

> Adopt the customs and constitution of the country in which you live, but also be careful to follow the religion of your fathers. As well as you can you must carry both burdens. It is not easy because, on the one hand, people make it hard for you to carry the burden of civil life because of your faithfulness to your religion and, on the other hand, the climate of the times makes keeping religious law harder than it need be in some respects. Nevertheless you must try. Stand fast in the place you have been allocated by Providence and submit to everything that happens to you as you were commanded long ago by your law giver. I do not understand how those who are part of the household of Jacob can with a good conscience not fully observe the Jewish law.[1]

Thus despite Mendelssohn's recognition of the common links between Judaism and other faiths, he followed the traditions of his ancestors and advocated the retention of the distinctive features of the Jewish faith. By combining philosophical theism and Jewish tradition-alism, Mendelssohn sought to transcend the constrictions of ghetto life and enter the mainstream of Western European culture as an observant Jew. To bring about the modernization of Jewish life, Mendelssohn also translated the Pentateuch into German so that Jews would be able to learn the language of the country in which they lived, and he spearheaded a commentary on scripture (the *Biur*) which combined Jewish scholarship with secular thought.

The ideas of the *Haskalah* (Jewish Enlightenment) were promoted by the journal *Ha-Meassef* (*The Gatherer*) launched by a group of Prussian *maskilim* (followers of the Enlightenment) in 1783 known as 'The Friends of the Hebrew Language'. Leading thinkers including Mendelssohn contributed to this journal, and the movement specialized in producing books in Hebrew on Jewish history and other subjects. In addition, they founded Jewish schools with a mixed curriculum of Jewish studies and secular topics. Over 200 schools were created in Austria, and over 100 in Galicia. From its German centre the *Haskalah* spread to other parts of Europe by the 1830s, especially to Poland and Russia. Increasingly the movement was attacked by the Orthodox establishment. Yet, by the mid-nineteenth century, the *Haskalah* was firmly entrenched in Eastern Europe, particularly in Vilna. The *maskilim*, however, were not typical of the Jewish masses. Many lived isolated lives because of their support of the Austrian and Russian government's efforts to reform Jewish lives. In addition, because they were virulently critical of traditional Judaism, they were regarded with suspicion and hostility.

The Enlightenment brought about major changes

in Jewish life. No longer were Jews insulated from non-Jewish currents of culture and thought, and this transformation of Jewish existence led many Jews to seek a modernization of Jewish worship. At the beginning of the nineteenth century the Jewish financier and communal leader Israel Jacobson initiated a programme of reform. He founded a boarding school for boys in Seesen, Westphalia in 1801, and subsequently established other schools throughout the kingdom. In these new foundations general subjects were taught by Christian teachers while a Jewish instructor gave lessons about Judaism. The consistory under Jacobson's leadership also introduced external reforms to the Jewish worship service including choral singing, hymns and addresses, and prayers in German. In 1810 Jacobson built the first Reform temple next to the school which was dedicated in the presence of Christian clergy and dignitaries.

After Napoleon's defeat Jacobson moved to Berlin where he sought to put these principles into practice by founding the Berlin temple. In Hamburg in 1818 a Reform temple was opened in which a number of innovations were made to the liturgy including prayers and sermons in German as well as choral singing and organ music. The central aim of these early reformers was to adapt Jewish worship to contemporary aesthetic standards. For these innovators, the informality of the traditional worship service seemed foreign and undignified, and they therefore insisted on greater decorum, more unions in prayer, a choir, hymns and music responses as well as alterations in prayers and the length of the service.

Yet for some Jews influenced by the Romantic

movement, these modifications were insufficient. Two of Moses Mendelssohn's daughters, for example, became Christian converts as did Henriette Herz and Rachel Varnhagen whose literary salons in Berlin were attended by leading German intellectuals. These women longed for a faith which would provide sublime devotion and mystical bliss.

Such Romantic concern also generated a new intellectual development within post-Enlightenment Jewry – the establishment of a Society for the Culture and Academic Study of Judaism. This discipline encouraged the systematic study of history and a new respect for historical fact. The purpose of this new approach to the past was to gain a true understanding of the origins of the Jewish tradition in the history of western civilization, and in this quest the philosophy of Hegel had an important influence. In 1824, however, the society collapsed and several of its members such as the poet Henrich Heine and the historian of law Eduard Gans converted to Christianity to advance their careers.

In time a more radical approach to the Jewish past was taken by a number of German rabbis who had been influenced by the Enlightenment. In this undertaking the achievements of Jewish scholars such as Leopold Zunz had a profound impact. As this new movement began to grow, Orthodox authorities vigorously attacked its leadership and ideals. In 1838, for example, when Abraham Geiger was appointed as second rabbi of Breslau, the chief rabbi of the city, Solomon Tiktin, denounced him as a radical. According to Tiktin, anyone who does not subscribe to the inviolable and absolute truth of tradition could not serve with him. Tiktin's allies joined in this protest and declared Geiger unfit. In 1842 Tiktin published a tract in which he insisted on the validity of Jewish law and the authority of the rabbinic tradition. In response Geiger's supporters produced a defence of religious reform.

During this period Reform Judaism spread to other countries, but it was in Frankfurt that Reform became most radical. In 1842 the Society of the Friends of Reform was founded and published a proclamation justifying their innovative approach to tradition. In the declaration of their principles, the society declared that they recognized the possibility of unlimited progress in the Jewish faith and rejected the authority of the legal code as well as the belief in messianic redemption. Further, members of the society considered circumcision a barbaric rite which should be eliminated. A similar group, the Association for the Reform of Judaism, was founded in Berlin in 1844 and under the leadership of Samuel Holdheim called for major changes in the Jewish tradition.

In 1844 the first Reform synod took place at Brunswick in which the participants advocated the formulation of a Jewish creed and the modification of sabbath and dietary laws as well as the traditional liturgy. This consultation was followed by another conference in 1845 in Frankfurt which recommended that petitions for the return to Israel and the restoration of the Jewish state be omitted from the prayerbook. In 1846 a third synod took place at Breslau and discussed sabbath observance. Though these reformers upheld the rabbinic ordinances against work on the sabbath, they stated that the *talmudic* injunctions regarding the boundary for walking on the sabbath were no longer binding. Further, they stipulated that the second day observance of festivals should be eliminated.

The revolution of 1848 and its aftermath brought about the cessation of these conferences, and nearly a generation passed before reformers met again to formulate a common policy. In 1868 24 rabbis assembled at Cassel to lay the foundations for a synodal conference of rabbis, scholars and communal leaders. In the following year over 80 congregations were represented when this gathering met at Leipzig. Two years later another synod took place in Augusburg which dealt with pressing theological and practical problems.

The first signs of Reform appeared in the United States in 1824 when a small group of congregants in Charleston, South Carolina, attempted to introduce some of the reforms of Germany's Hamburg temple into synagogue worship. In the period preceding and following the revolution of 1848, there was an outpouring of Jews including some reformers from Germany to the United States. Many of these immigrants settled in New York. By 1842 there were three German congregations in New York City. Some years later Congregation Emanuel was organized and introduced various reforms in worship. Among these German newcomers were several Reform rabbis who had taken part in the early European Reform synods and were anxious to initiate a policy of Reform in the New World.

These developments in Europe and elsewhere brought about major changes in Jewish life. No longer were Jews confined to a ghetto lifestyle. Instead, modernizers were intent on transforming traditional Jewish belief and practice. In their view, the Orthodox way of life was no longer adequate for contemporary Jewry. Instead, they believed Jews should integrate into the societies in which they lived and accommodate themselves to the main currents of contemporary culture. Joining together in a series of synods they formulated a common policy. In their quest to overcome previous disabilities, they forged a new approach to the Jewish faith, distancing themselves from the past.

5

REFORMING JUDAISM

Reform Judaism offered Jews an opportunity to assimilate into the cultures in which they lived. No longer were Jews confined to a ghetto existence – the Enlightenment had freed them from the fetters of the past. Instead a new age had dawned; in the view of modernizers the Jewish faith should adapt to changed circumstances. By this means, Jewry would be able to overcome social disabilities of previous centuries. In the United States, the Reform movement gained a considerable following, and by the end of the nineteenth century reformers had reformulated the central tenets of the faith.

REFORM JUDAISM

Orthodox critics viewed the attitude of reformers with horror. The most eloquent critic of Reform was Samson Raphael Hirsch, the founder of Neo-Orthodoxy in the middle of the nineteenth century. In his view, the steps taken by reformers were heretical. There is, he believed, only one form of Judaism: Orthodoxy. As he declared in 'Religion Allied to Progress':

Judaism does not know any varieties of Judaism. It conceives Judaism as one and indivisible. It does not know a Mosaic, prophetic and rabbinic Judaism, nor Orthodox and Liberal Judaism. It only knows Judaism and non-Judaism. It does not know Orthodox and Liberal Jews. It does indeed know conscientious and indifferent Jews, good Jews, bad Jews or baptised Jews.[1]

Reformers, however, claimed that their interpretation of the faith was legitimate. In their view, Judaism has always undergone change, and their innovations, they believed, were no different from the modifications that had taken place in the past.

With the emigration of vast numbers of European Jews at the end of the nineteenth century, Reform Judaism became an important movement in the New World. Under the leadership of Issac Mayer Wise, a Bohemian rabbi who settled first in Cincinnati, Ohio, Reform Judaism established an institutional framework. After several abortive attempts at rabbinic union, the first Conference of American Reform Rabbis took place in Philadelphia in 1869; this was followed in 1873 by the founding of the Union of American Hebrew Congregations. Two years later Wise established the Hebrew Union College, the first Reform rabbinical seminary on American soil.

In 1885 the principles of Reform Judaism were set out by a gathering of Reform rabbis in Pittsburgh, Pennsylvania. Their deliberations resulted in the adoption of a formal set of principles: the Pittsburgh Platform. In contrast with Maimonides' principles of the Jewish faith, this document emphasized that modern Judaism should distance itself from the beliefs of previous centuries:

> First ... We hold that Judaism presents the highest recognition of the God-idea as taught in our holy scriptures and developed and spiritualized by the Jewish teachers in accordance with the moral and philosophical progress of their respective ages ...

> Second ... We hold that the modern discoveries of scientific researches in the domains of nature and history are not antagonistic to the doctrines of Judaism, the Bible reflecting the primitive ideas of its own age and at times clothing its conception of divine providence and justice dealing with man in miraculous narratives.

> Third ... Today we accept as binding only the moral laws and maintain only such ceremonies as elevate and sanctify our lives, but reject all such as are not adapted to the views and habits of modern civilization.

> Fourth ... We hold that all such Mosaic and rabbinical laws as regulate diet, priestly purity and dress origi-nated in ages and under the influence of ideas altogether foreign to our present mental and spiritual state ... Their observance in our day is apt rather to obstruct than to further modern spiritual elevation.

> Fifth ... We consider ourselves no longer a nation but a religious community, and therefore expect neither a

return to Palestine, nor a sacrificial worship under the administration of the sons of Aaron, nor the restoration of any of the laws concerning the Jewish state.

Sixth ... We recognize in Judaism a progressive religion, ever striving to be in accord with the postulates of reason ... We acknowledge that the spirit of broad humanity of our age is our ally in the fulfilment of our mission, and therefore we extend the hand of fellowship to all who co-operate with us in the establishment of the reign of truth and righteousness among men.

Seventh ... We reassert the doctrine of Judaism, that the soul of man is immortal ... We reject as ideas not rooted in Judaism the belief both in bodily resurrection and in *Gehenna* and Eden, as abodes for everlasting punishment or reward.

Eighth ... In full accord with the spirit of Mosaic legislation, which strives to regulate the relations between rich and poor, we deem it our duty to participate in the great task of modern times, to solve on the basis of justice and righteousness the problems presented by the contrasts and evils of the present organization of society.[2]

In his address to the conference, the chairman Kaufmann Kohler declared that their purpose was to show that Judaism must be modernized in order to embrace the findings of scientific research as well as comparative religion and biblical criticism. As we have seen, the Platform itself begins with the statement that Judaism presents the highest conception of God. In this connection the conference spoke of the Bible as the most potent instrument of religious and moral instruction. Yet, the participants decreed that they recognized as binding only the moral commandments as well as those rituals which they viewed as spiritually uplifting. Laws regulating diet, priestly purity and dress were rejected as anachronistic. The belief in a personal Messiah was eliminated and replaced by a messianic hope for the establishing of a kingdom of justice and peace for humanity. The reformers also asserted that Judaism is a progressive religion. Regarding the afterlife, the participants subscribed to a belief in the immortality of the soul rather than the traditional doctrines of bodily resurrection and reward and punishment in the hereafter. As a conclusion to this document, the delegates proclaimed their commitment to engage in social action. This statement of religious beliefs together with the rabbinical and congregational organizations of Reform Judaism founded in the late nineteenth century provided a framework for the growth and development of Reform Judaism in the next century.

Fifty years after the Pittsburgh meeting of 1885, the Jewish world had undergone major changes: America was the centre of the diaspora; Zionism had become a vital force in Jewish life; Hitler was in power. The Columbus Platform of the Reform movement of 1937 reflected a new approach to Reform Judaism. Again, the Reformers stressed their commitment to a belief in God 'who rules the world through law and love'. The belief in revelation was affirmed: both the written and oral *Torah* were viewed as containing a depository of permanent spiritual ideals. Nonetheless, 'each age has the obligation to adapt the teachings of the *Torah* to its basic needs'.[3]

Although the Pittsburgh Platform rejected the return to Palestine, the Columbus Platform adopted a more positive outlook:

> In the rehabilitation of Palestine, the land hallowed by memories and hopes, we behold the promise of renewed life for many of our brethren. We affirm the obligation of all Jewry to aid in its upbuilding as a Jewish homeland by endeavouring to make it not only a haven of refuge for the oppressed but also a centre of Jewish culture and spiritual life.[4]

After the Second World War, Reform Judaism continued to develop. On the far right of the movement a number of rabbis advocated a personalist basis for religious faith. Other thinkers, however, conceived of God in a less personal way. Rabbi Roland Gittelsohn, for example, rabbi of temple Israel in Boston, expressed a view held by others: 'I do not conceive of God as a Person but as an active spiritual seed of the universe – the Energy, the Power, the Force, the Direction, the Thrust ... in which the universe and mind find their meaning.'[5] In line with both the Pittsburgh and Columbus Platforms, the movement was united in rejecting the doctrine of *Torah MiSinai*. As Maurice Eisendrath, the President of the Union of American Reform Rabbis, stated: 'God is a living God – not a God who revealed himself and his word once and for all times at Sinai and speaks no more.'[6]

Despite adopting a more conservative stance towards *halakhah*, the movement discussed the issue of rabbinic participation in interfaith marriages. Although a resolution against such participation was passed in 1909, a growing number of rabbis subsequently participated in such ceremonies. Of greater consequence was the decision taken in 1983 by the Central Conference of American Rabbis expanding the determination of Jewishness to include patrilineal as well as matrilineal descent. By altering Jewish law in this way, the Reform movement defined as Jews individuals whom the other branches of Judaism regard as Gentiles. This means that neither these persons nor their offspring can be accepted as Jews by either Orthodox or Conservative Judaism.

In 1971 the Central Conference of American Rabbis sponsored a study of the nature of the Reform movement. Published in 1971, *Rabbi and Synagogue in American Judaism* provides an overview of the state of Reform belief and practice in the later half of the twentieth century. According to this survey, Jewish consciousness was identified by most Reform Jewish congregants in terms of living a moral life. Although Jewish identification was an important factor in the lives of most Reform Jews, many declared that they remained Jews simply because it is the most convenient thing to do. Even the most traditional were not particularly observant. More had a family Thanksgiving dinner, for example, than observed the High Holy Days at home. Almost as many exchanged Christmas gifts as attended Friday night services. In addition 17 per cent stated that they believed in God 'in the more or less traditional sense of the term'; 49 per cent qualified their belief in terms of their own religious views; 8 per cent maintained that they were non-religious believers; 21 per cent said they were agnostics; and 4 per cent identified themselves as atheists.

In 1976 the Reform movement produced the San Francisco Platform; like the Pittsburgh and Columbus Platforms, this declaration seeks to provide a unifying framework which would bring a sense of order into the movement. Although it avoids taking a theological position, it affirms God's reality without defining what is meant by this expression. The *Torah*, it explains, resulted from 'the relationship between God and the Jewish people' and Israel was viewed as an 'uncommon union of faith and peoplehood'. *Mitzvot* are interpreted as 'claims made upon us'.[7] Although vague and equivocal, the San Francisco Platform nonetheless did provide a sense of unity despite the divisions within modern Reform Jewry.

More recently the Reform movement produced a new statement of principles. The onset of the twenty-first century suggested to the leaders of Reform Judaism that a new set of principles was needed. The rise in mixed marriage and the inclusion of those of patrilineal descent had changed the demographics of the Reform movement. In addition, the acceptance of gay and lesbian Jews and the quest for a more spiritual ideology had significantly affected the composition and nature of Reform community. Organized around the themes of God, *Torah* and Israel, the Pittsburgh Principles affirm the reality and oneness of God, although the movement stressed that Reform Jews differ in their understanding of the divine. Similarly, the statement makes a range of affirmations about the *Torah* and Israel. Yet, despite the move towards a more traditional approach, the Pittsburgh Principles stress that despite reverence for the Jewish heritage, individuals are free to embrace those aspects of the tradition which they find spiritually meaningful. In this respect, the Pittsburgh Principles remain faithful to the ideology of the past. In its commentary on this new statement, the Central Conference of American Rabbis (CCAR) stressed that its series of affirmations do not bind the movement to confessional belief: 'That a movement affirms a given statement or value does not mean that those who cannot or do not believe it are, ipso facto, outside the movement.' With regard to belief in God, for example, the CCAR states:

> There is room in Reform Judaism ... for a variety of understandings of God's reality, including individuals who are not sure whether they believe in God or think that they do not believe in God. Jews who are members of a movement that affirms God's reality suggest by their membership that they are willing to continue to wrestle with that reality as befits their membership in the People of Israel, from the Hebrew Yisrael which the *Torah* defines (Genesis 32:29) as 'the one who wrestles with God and human beings has prevailed'.[8]

Concerning *mitzvot*, the CCAR advises:

Since its inception, the Reform Movement has wrestled with the classic notion of God commanding us – it seems so frontal, so authoritarian, so hierarchial. But if God is in dialogue with us, perhaps we hear God's commands as though God were calling out to us, in words that a beloved human being in our lives might use, 'It is very important to me that you do this' – awaiting our response. We may respond to many of these calls by taking on these sacred obligations, building them into our lives; to others, we may respond, 'We need to dialogue more.' To others we may respond, 'I cannot do this act – in terms of my present moral and communal understanding it seems meaningless, or even wrong.' And perhaps God responds as our beloved might: 'Let's keep the conversation going.'[9]

Such individualism is far distant from the inflexible Orthodoxy of the past. Throughout its history, Reform Judaism has categorically ejected Jewish absolutism. In its place, it has fostered individual freedom and personal responsibility. Yet, as a consequence Reform Jews have distanced themselves from both the belief system of Judaism and the *Code of Jewish Law*. Liberated from the constraints of ghetto life, Reform Jews seek to chart their own paths through the tradition. Even the most observant do not live in accordance with the myriad of commandments laid down in scripture and expanded by the sages. It is no wonder that the ultra-Orthodox are adamant that Reform Judaism is an inauthentic interpretation of the Jewish way of life. Committed to the doctrine of

Torah MiSinai, they insist that only Orthodoxy fulfils the criterion of Jewishness. Reform Judaism, they assert, is a heretical sect, devoid of holiness and reverence for God.

6

THE MIDDLE WAY –
CONSERVATIVE JUDAISM

In the nineteenth century Reform Judaism constituted a major departure from the past: after centuries of discrimination and persecution, Jews believed that they stood on the threshold of a new age. Yet some modernizers were concerned that the Reform movement was far too radical. Pre-eminent among such critics, Zacharias Frankel broke ranks with other Reformers. An advocate of moderate reform, he was committed to a historically evolving dynamic Judaism. The aim of such an approach, he believed, would be to uncover the origins of the Jewish people's national spirit and the collective will. Both the past as enshrined in tradition and the present as embodied in the religious consciousness of the people should determine the nature of Jewish life.

THE CONSERVATIVE MOVEMENT

In 1845 Frankel left the Reform rabbinical conference in Frankfurt because a majority of the participants had voted that there was no need to use Hebrew in the Jewish worship service. At this synod, one of the Reform leaders,

Abraham Geiger, maintained that since Hebrew was simply a national element in the service which Reform Judaism sought to replace with universal symbols it could be eliminated. In response, Frankel stated that Hebrew is a vital historical feature of the Jewish heritage – it is the sacred tongue in which Jews have expressed their beliefs and ideals through the centuries. Although he agreed with other reformers that Judaism needed to be revised, he had a different view concerning the legitimate criteria for religious change. Nonetheless, he broke with Orthodoxy in asserting that the oral law was rabbinic in origin, that the *halakhah* had evolved over time, and that the source of religious observance was not divine.

In 1854 Frankel became the head of the Jewish Theological Seminary in Breslau which eventually became the most important rabbinical college in Europe. Frankel insisted that the seminary was not to be identified with the Reform movement, yet neither was it to be Orthodox in orientation. Committed to free inquiry, Frankel rejected Samson Raphael Hirsch's request that the seminary endorse the traditional doctrine of *Torah MiSinai*; instead he stressed the importance of historical research into the origins of rabbinic teachings.

In the United States, a similar approach to the tradition was adopted by a number of leading figures. The German-born *hazzan* of Congregation *Mikveh* Israel, Isaac Lesser, for example, pioneered the introduction of the sermon in English and advocated liturgical change. Although a staunch traditionalist in other respects, he co-operated with Isaac Mayer Wise in attempting to organize rabbinic and congregational union. Two other scholars,

Marcus Jastrow and Alexander Kohut, also advocated change to the worship service. When the Reform rabbinate published the Pittsburgh Platform in 1885, Kohut took issue with Kaufmann Kohler, the principal author of the document, and together with another conservative reformer of this period, Sabato Morais, encouraged the creation of a rabbinic school dedicated to the knowledge and practice of historical Judaism.

In 1887 the Jewish Theological Seminary was founded by Morais, Mendes and Kohut, as well as a number of prominent laymen. In 1902 the Cambridge scholar Solomon Schechter became its president. It was Schechter's desire to combine Jewish traditionalism with a commitment to the scientific study of Judaism. Yet despite his adherence to traditional practices, the Union of Orthodox Rabbis issued a writ of excommunication against the seminary in 1904. In response, Schechter began to delineate the nature of what came to be regarded as Conservative Judaism. Disdainfully, Schecter rejected both Reform and Orthodoxy; instead, he emphasized the importance of traditional rituals, customs and observances, as well as belief, while simultaneously stressing the need for a historical perspective.

In contrast with the Orthodox, Schechter admired modern scientific biblical scholarship. In line with contemporary biblical criticism, he maintained that the Pentateuch is not of divine origin. In February 1913 a union of 22 congregations was founded, committed to maintaining the Jewish tradition in its historical continuity. As Conservative Judaism expanded in the 1920s and 1930s, a degree of uniformity emerged in congregational worship: services normally commenced late Friday evening and early Saturday morning; men were required to wear head coverings; prayer shawls were obligatory on sabbath morning; rabbis conducted the service and preached sermons in English; prayer-books other than the *Union Prayer Book* of the Reform movement were used; many congregants joined the rabbi for afternoon study. Further, many synagogues had organs, mixed choirs and family pews, as well as *minyans* that met three times a day for prayer.

From its beginnings in the nineteenth century, Conservatism emphasized that East European immigrants should adjust to the social, economic and cultural conditions of America while preserving their Jewish identity. In advocating this approach, Conservative Jews viewed the Jewish faith as an evolving organism that remained spiritually vibrant by adjusting to the environmental and cultural conditions of the present. In consequence, Conservative Jewish thinkers strove to preserve those elements of the tradition which they believed to be spiritually meaningful while simultaneously setting aside those observances which actually hindered the continued development of Judaism. Such obsolete practices were not abrogated, but simply ignored. In a similar spirit, Conservative Jews, in contrast with the Orthodox, felt no compulsion to accept theological doctrines which they believed were outmoded.

Like Reform Judaism, Conservatism advances a number of central theological tenets while leaving scope for personal interpretation. Regarding the doctrine of God, Conservative writers have generally subscribed to the Orthodox understanding of God as omnipotent, omniscient and all-good. God is hence viewed as a transcendent person who gave the *Torah* to Israel. Yet in contrast with Orthodox Judaism, there is considerable uncertainty about this process of divine disclosure. Unlike Orthodox writers who conceive of revelation as verbal in nature and Reform theologians who conceive of the *Torah* as the product of human reflection, the Conservative movement has generally attempted to bridge these two positions. As to what constitutes a divine–human encounter, Conservative Jews vary: some maintain that human beings correctly recorded the divine will as disclosed at Sinai; others contend that the writers of scripture were divinely inspired. Despite such differences, most Conservative thinkers recognize that there was greater divine involvement in the *Torah* compared with the other books of the Hebrew Bible even though they reject the Orthodox belief that God literally revealed the *Torah* in its entirety to Moses on Mount Sinai.

Regarding *halakhah*, most Conservative thinkers emphasize the importance of keeping traditional Jewish law, including dietary observances, sabbath, festival and liturgical prescriptions and ethical precepts. Nonetheless, Conservative writers have encouraged change and renewal. On the whole they have emphasized the historical importance of the Jewish heritage. Guided by such an approach to Jewish law, the Conservative movement resorted to what Schechter called the 'conscience of the Catholic Israel' in determining the status of both biblical and rabbinic law. In the early years of the movement, a number of leaders urged Conservative Jews to reach consensual agreement. As a consequence 'Catholic Israel' came to signify the vast majority of the membership of Conservative synagogues. Further, a body of representative rabbis selected by the rabbinical body of the movement established a Committee on Jewish Law; later this body was expanded into a Committee on Jewish Law on Standards. This Committee rules on issues of Jewish law in the light of past needs and present conditions.

Unless this Committee makes unanimous recommendations, congregational rabbis are at liberty to rely on their own authority; although this resulted in charges of inconsistency, this approach allowed individual rabbis freedom of decision-making. In establishing its attitude to *halakhah*, Conservative Judaism stressed that *halakhic* change does not emanate from God's revelation on Mount Sinai, but from Catholic Israel. The Conservative movement thus based its decisions on human reflection rather than God's will. In expounding this approach the Conservative movement has in general viewed the main outlines of the Jewish legal system as binding, but has permitted individuals to fill in the amount of detail they wish to follow: this is the sphere where personal choice is fundamental.

Regarding authority, the Conservative movement has adopted a range of positions. The most traditional view asserts that God revealed himself to Moses and at other times in the history of the nation; these revelations, however, were recorded by human beings and as such provide a variety of interpretations of this encounter with God. Nonetheless, the revelation to Moses was the fullest and most public disclosure – this is the most authori-

tative record of God's will. From Sinai on, Jewish law
and theology are to be conceived as individual percep-
tions: hence the authority of Jewish law is based first on
the fact of God's revelation, and second on the amplifi-
cation of this legislation by reliable rabbinic commentary.
Modifications of the law are acceptable, but only with
extreme caution. According to this position, all the laws
of the *Torah* are authoritative in character – yet there is
an acknowledgement that divine law is mediated through
human comprehension. In this light, the historical investigation of Judaism is a viable enterprise since the
tradition is perceived as subject to historical change. On
such a view, God spoke at Sinai – his will is authoritative for all time. Yet such a belief does not preclude a
historical and literary analysis of the biblical text since it
was written down by human hands.

An alternative understanding of divine authority
is based on a number of different assumptions. On
this view, the *Torah* was composed by human beings
at various times and places; hence the *Torah* contains
diverse documents, laws and ideas. Nonetheless, those
who wrote down these words were divinely inspired and
their words carry the insight and authority of God. In
this light, Jewish laws and ideas can be altered since the
Torah is a combination of divine inspiration on the one
hand, and human articulation on the other. Moreover,
divine inspiration did not occur once and for all at Sinai
– it continues in the form of new interpretations for
future generations. Changes to the law are permissible,
but they must take place through rabbinic decisions and
communal custom.

A further notion of authority within the Conservative movement is that revelation should be understood as the disclosure of God himself, rather than a series of propositions. It is not revelation or inspiration which takes place, but instead the meeting of God and human beings. On this view, the *Torah* is a record of the human response to God. Jewish law thus has authority for the Jewish people because Jews are members of a covenanted community. As such, they have obligations to follow God's law. However, since the *Torah* was composed by human beings, it is necessary to employ the techniques of biblical scholarship to uncover the origins and meanings of scripture. Further, since the Bible is a human product it reflects the social and cultural milieu of its authors. It follows that Jewry today must alter the tradition so that it most effectively expresses God's will in the modern world. Finally, this understanding of God's encounter with the Jewish people as a whole is fundamental. Changes in laws of the Jewish faith must be made by rabbis on behalf of the entire community rather than by specific individuals independent of the rabbinic establishment.

We can see, therefore, that despite its reverence for the Jewish tradition, Conservative Judaism has severed itself from Orthodoxy. Like Reform Judaism, it has distanced itself from the traditional understanding of divine revelation. The *Torah* is perceived as a composite work containing various strands of tradition, dating from different periods in the history of ancient Israel. As a result, there is uncertainty about the status of both Jewish belief and observance. Some traditionalists assert that scriptural and rabbinic law remains authoritative for the community; others press for *halakhic* change. Regarding the doctrine of God, some Conservative thinkers believe in a personal, supernatural deity who is active in human history; others maintain that God should be understood in non-personal terms. Similarly, Conservative thought is divided concerning the doctrine of revelation. Some traditionalists believe that God revealed the *Torah* to Israel even though they do not accept that every word in the *Torah* is of divine origin; others believe in the doctrine of divine inspiration, holding to a notion of progressive encounter.

The same lack of agreement is found in the sphere of *halakhic* interpretation. In general Conservative Jews accept that the *halakhah* has a pivotal role to play in the modern world. Yet within the movement there are widely discrepant patterns of observance. Officially Conservative Judaism insists that its members uphold the *mitzvot* and lead a life based on Jewish law. In reality, however, few Conservative laypeople live up to this ideal. Moreover, the movement has officially sanctioned practices which deviate from the tradition. For example, Conservative Jews are permitted to use electricity on the sabbath and festivals; the observance of the second day of Passover, *Shavuot* and *Sukkot* are regarded as optional; Conservative Jews are permitted to discard skull-caps outside the synagogue; women are not obliged to cover their hair or go to the mikveh. Hence there is considerable ambiguity about acceptable patterns of observance within the movement: no uniformity exists, nor is it conceivable that a coherent Jewish lifestyle could emerge given the lack of agreement about the essential features of the faith.

Like Reform Judaism, Conservative Judaism thus constitutes a radical departure from the tradition. Even though more moderate than Reform, the Conservative movement has consciously distanced itself from both belief and observance. The rejection of the doctrine of *Torah MiSinai* provides a basis for the elimination of those laws which, in the view of Conservative scholars and leaders, are no longer relevant in the modern age. In official statements of its principles, Conservative Judaism has also sanctioned beliefs which deviate from the tradition. As a consequence, the traditional Jewish way of life has been eroded by those anxious to reconstruct Judaism for the modern age.

7

RECONSTRUCTING JUDAISM

Both Reform and Conservative Judaism have distanced themselves from Orthodoxy – these modernist movements have abandoned many of the central principles of traditional Judaism including the doctrine of *Torah MiSinai*. As a consequence, Reform and Conservative Jews have ceased to observe the multifarious ordinances of the faith. Yet, there are even more radical movements within the contemporary Jewish community. Reconstructionist Judaism, for example, advances a naturalistic form of Judaism, devoid of theistic belief.

RECONSTRUCTIONIST JUDAISM

When my wife and I interviewed two Humanist Jews who had previously been members of a Reconstructionist movement, they explained their perplexity about the movement:

> **Edie:** Then I thought that the philosophy of humanism means you shouldn't belong to a little group. You belong to the world. We're all humans. I really believed that, but no one else in the world felt that way. I felt I

was giving up something to be this universalist – and I was totally alone. Well that didn't feel too great!

Jay: Then we went to the Reconstructionists.

Edie: And that seemed to be it! They said that God is the human being's ability to actualize himself and become all that it is possible to become. That was the Reconstructionist definition of God.

Jay: At that time, it felt very comfortable ...

Edie: Then we started going to Reconstructionist study groups – and boy were they observant! They said all the traditional prayers. I kept asking the rabbi why we kept using this God-talk if it didn't refer to God. I felt I was doing mental gymnastics all the time. In services, every time we got to the word 'God', I kept saying, 'My ability to actualize myself and become all that it is possible to become' ... and it didn't fit! I kept saying this to the rabbi and he got annoyed. so after a bit we quit going and then we dropped out.[1]

Despite such criticisms, a significant number of Jews have been attracted to Reconstructionism. Unlike the Reform and Conservative movements, Reconstructionism emerged out of the thinking of an individual Jewish scholar. Born in Lithuania, Mordecai Kaplan was a Professor at the Jewish Theological Seminary. During the 1910s and 1920s Kaplan engaged in wide-ranging congregational activity. According to some scholars,

Reconstructionism began in 1922 when Kaplan initiated a programme of reconstructing Judaism to meet the demands of contemporary Jewish life; another interpretation traces the origins of the movement to the publication of Kaplan's *Judaism as a Civilization* in 1934.

In any event, *Judaism as a Civilization* provided the basis for Reconstrucitonist ideology. In this work, Kaplan began by assessing the main religious groupings of American Jewry. In his opinion, Reform had correctly acknowledged the evolving character of Judaism as a religious system, yet it ignored the social basis of Jewish identity as well as the organic character of the community. Neo-Orthodoxy, on the other hand, recognized Judaism as a way of life and provided an intensive programme of Jewish education. Nonetheless, it mistakenly viewed the Jewish religion as static. In contrast, Conservative Judaism was committed to the scientific study of the development of the Jewish faith while upholding the unity of the Jewish people. Yet Conservative Judaism was too closely bound to Jewish law and thus unable to respond to changing circumstances. All of these movements, he believed, failed to accommodate the Jewish heritage to the modern age; what was needed, Kaplan insisted, was a definition of Judaism as an evolving civilization: hence the title of his book.

The central principle of Reconstructionism is that Judaism is an evolving religious civilization: in the biblical period the Jews constituted a people; later they became a religious congregation; eventually they entered the rabbinic era when the legal system ruled their lives; in modern times individual Jews are free to adapt the tradition to their own needs. Because of this continual development, ideas about God, humanity, sin, miracles, laws, prayer and the afterlife have all undergone considerable change. In Kaplan's view, Judaism is therefore more than a religious denomination; it is a total civilization embracing art, music, language, folkways and customs whose purpose is to ensure the survival of the Jewish nation.

Within this framework, Reconstructionists have adopted a humanistic and naturalistic understanding of the nature of the divine based on Kaplan's teachings. Kaplan was a humanist because he discerned the presence of God in human experience: human potential and striving to improve life reflect the power of God. Kaplan also found evidence of design in the universe because nature follows specific laws. In his opinion, the regularity of nature was devised to enable human beings to achieve their highest goals. In this light, Kaplan believed that faith in God should be grounded in scientific knowledge and on a faith in humanity.

Such a humanistic perspective is based on a radically new definition of God as the power that makes for human salvation and fulfilment. In his works, Kaplan repeatedly expressed his faith that human beings have the capacity to strive for such ideals as justice, truth, goodness and peace. Just as gravity is an invisible force in nature, he asserted, so there is a power in human beings which makes humans strive for perfection. That power is what we call 'God'. Reconstructionism thus does not teach that God is a person residing in heaven. Such a notion, Kaplan believed, is a childlike fantasy. It is a mistake to strive to experience God through mysticism, nor should we think of God as a miracle-worker or judge. In this connection Reconstructionists insist that God, as defined in Kaplan's system, is limited. According to Reconstructionist Judaism, God's power extends only to certain spheres, yet Reconstructionists believe that one day God's spirit will fill the entire world. Our task as humans and as Jews is to bring about the realization of such a utopian vision.

Turning to the doctrine of revelation, Reconstructionism differs markedly from Orthodox Judaism. Accepting the findings of modern biblical scholars who view the *Torah* as composite, Kaplan stressed that the Bible is not a record of God's dealing with his chosen people; rather it reflects the Jewish search for God. Hence whenever a great teaching or moral truth is uncovered in scripture, this is a revelation of God's will. As a consequence of this view, Reconstructionists do not regard Jewish law as holy and unchanging. Since the Jewish community can no longer enforce an acceptance of *mitzvot*, it is misleading to retain the legal terminology of the past. In place of traditional language, Reconstructionists utilize the terms 'folkways' and 'customs' to designate traditional observances, expressions which reflect the fact that throughout history all peoples have created their sacred events, holy days and religious objects. In the same way Jewry has its heroes (patriarchs, Moses, prophets, rabbis), sacred events (birth, marriage, death), holy days (sabbath, *Rosh Hashanah*, *Yom Kippur*, pilgrim festivals) and holy objects (*Torah*, *tefillin*, prayer shawls). Such folkways bring Jews closer to God, help individuals to lead more meaningful lives, and bring the community together as a united people.

In Kaplan's view, folkways and customs help to sustain the Jewish nation and enrich the spiritual life of Jewry. Yet Kaplan argued that such observances should be accepted voluntarily; in the modern world there is no role for coercive authority. In this regard, Kaplan endorsed the concept of democratic decision-making in determining which laws are relevant for the community. The past, he declared, should have a vote, but not a veto. In this spirit Kaplan believed that the Jewish legal code should be consulted, but previous rulings should not determine contemporary practices. For Kaplan, anach-ronistic laws as well as those regulations which conflict with the highest ideals of Judaism have no place in a modern Code of Jewish Law unless new meaning can be given to them. Further, Kaplan stressed the importance of formulating new customs to take the place of those that had ceased to give meaning to contemporary Jewish life. Initially it was feared that such freedom of choice might lead to anarchy, but Kaplan suggested that such a difficulty could be avoided if legal guides were produced by the movement – as a result the *Guide to Ritual Usage* was created in 1941. Such resources, he believed, should be perceived as guidelines rather than obligatory rules. In his opinion, it should be the people, rather than the rabbis, who determine appropriate patterns of observance.

One of the most important features of Reconstructionist ideology is its emphasis on Jewish peoplehood. For Kaplan, the purpose of Jewish civilization is to ensure the continuation of the group; moreover, in his view the *Torah* exists for the sake of the nation. It is a great *mitzvah* for any people to survive, create and flourish, he believed, but for the Jews this is an even greater obligation since the Jewish people were created in the image of God. The purpose of Reconstructionist Judaism is therefore to revive the Jewish people's will to identify with tradition. To promote this goal, Kaplan recommended that representatives of world Jewry gather together each year in Jerusalem to renew the sacred covenant. Yet, despite this focus on Jewish solidarity Kaplan did not believe the Jewish community was chosen by God – such an idea, he argued, is racist in character. In place of this notion Kaplan propagated the concept of mission. Hence Reconstructionists believe it is necessary to live in two spheres simultaneously as a Jew in secular society. It is the responsibility of modern Jewry to strengthen Judaism by blending together the positive elements of contemporary culture and the most important values of the Jewish heritage.

Despite Kaplan's endorsement of Zionism and his belief that a full Jewish life could only be led in Israel, Kaplan was a realist, recognizing that it was unlikely that most Jews would in fact settle in the Holy Land. As a consequence he rejected the standard Zionist conviction that Israel should be a religious state characterized by *Torah* Judaism. Instead he asserted that the Jewish homeland should be governed by spiritual principles in line with Ahad Ha-Am's teaching about spiritual ideals. According to Ahad Ha-Am, *Eretz Israel* should be a cultural and spiritual centre. Similarly Kaplan believed that the State of Israel could inspire world Jewry and draw the community back to tradition.

In accord with this policy, Kaplan endorsed the creation of community centres designed to bring together all the various factions within the Jewish population. Continually he urged Jews to establish organic communities, based like the *kehillot* of Europe on voluntary membership. These American *kehillot*, he argued, should include Jewish community councils or organizations to which all Jews would be encouraged to belong regardless of their religious and political differences. In line with this conception of communal life, Kaplan taught that the aim of religion is to bring fulfilment to the Jewish people as a whole rather than to its individual members. This could take place, he believed, only if religious principles were translated into action. Embracing this policy of social involvement, Reconstructionism from its beginnings engaged in social action.

Since its inception, the movement has produced liturgical resources reflecting its ideology. In these prayerbooks, Reconstructionists insisted on the validity of their perspective. Thus in the *New Haggadah*, the editors assert that all references to events, real or imaginary, in the exodus story which might conflict with the highest ethical ideals be omitted. In reply to the criticism that such a non-supernatural standpoint renders prayer a meaningless activity, Kaplan argued that worship should intensify one's Jewish consciousness. It should, he wrote, interpret the divine aspect of life as manifest in social idealism. It should emphasize the high worth of potentialities of the individual soul. The purpose of prayer is therefore to affirm one's commitment to an ongoing heritage that extols human values.

As far as the *Guide to Ritual Usage* is concerned, Reconstructionists emphasize that the legal system is no longer binding on all Jews. Rather the *Guide* extols Jewish observances as a means to group survival and the enhancement of human existence. According to Reconstructionist ideology, each Jew should be at liberty to determine which rituals and folkways should be practised. Such a liberal outlook provides individual Jews with a broad latitude in their departure from traditional law. The *Guide* explains the significance of a set of rituals for the various Jewish holidays and recommends their adoption, but it affirms that the ultimate criterion for deciding which observances should be retained is the self-fulfilment of the individual.

Thus, for example, the *Guide* suggests that work permitted on the sabbath includes all enjoyable activities which a person is unable to engage in during the week excluding the means of making a living. For Reconstructionists, what matters is not the ceremonial observance of the sabbath, but the extent to which these ceremonies help one to live and experience sabbath joy. Consistent with Kaplan's early writing, the *Guide* stresses that Jewish folkways should be observed if they enhance modern life – thus Reconstructionists seek to provide a social rationale, rather than a theological justification for obeying the commandments.

Reconstructionist Judaism constitutes a dramatic reconceptualization of Judaism, far removed from Orthodoxy. Although Reconstructionist Jews seek to find spiritual significance in the *sancta* of Jewish life, they reject the biblical and rabbinic conception of God. In their view, there is no personal deity who created the universe and exercises providential care for his creation. Instead, Reconstructionist Judaism emphasizes communal solidarity and religious observance. Adopting a non-supernaturalistic outlook, Reconstructionist Jews extol Jewish practices as the embodiment of their cultural heritage.

8

Radical Judaism

Not surprisingly, Orthodox Jews regard Reconstructionist Judaism, along with the other non-Orthodox branches of Judaism, as a danger to the faith. Their hostility, however, is not restricted to this new movement. Humanistic Judaism, an even more radical interpretation of Judaism, is the cause of grave concern. Like Reconstructionist Judaism, Jewish Humanism offers a non-theistic interpretation of the Jewish faith.

Humanistic Judaism

Originating in the 1960s in Detroit, Michigan, under the leadership of Sherwin Wine, Humanistic Judaism now numbers about 40,000 members in the United States, Europe and elsewhere. Distancing itself from the other branches of Judaism, this new movement extols the humanistic dimensions of the faith. Officially, it rejects any form of theistic belief; in its place, the movement stresses the importance of human reason:

> We believe in the value of human reason and in the reality of the world which reason discloses. The natural

universe stands on its own, requiring no supernatural intervention. We believe in the value of human existence and in the power of human beings to solve the problems both individually and collectively. Life should be directed to the satisfaction of human needs. Every person is entitled to life, dignity and freedom. We believe in the value of Jewish identity and in the survival of the Jewish people. Jewish history is a human story. Judaism, as the civilization of the Jews, is a human creation. Jewish identity is an ethnic reality. The civilization of the Jewish people embraces all manifestations of Jewish life, including Jewish languages, ethical traditions, historic memories, cultural heritage, and especially the emergence of the state of Israel in modern times. Judaism also embraces many belief systems and lifestyles. As the creation of the Jewish people in all ages, it is always changing. We believe in the value of a secular humanistic democracy for Israel and for all the nations of the world. Religion and state must be separate. The individual right to privacy and moral autonomy must be guaranteed. Equal rights must be granted to all, regardless of race, sex, creed or ethnic origins.[1]

In accordance with this philosophy of Judaism, the Federation of Secular Humanistic Jews advocated a new conception of Jewish identity. In answer to the question 'Who is a Jew?', the movement declared:

We the members of the International Federation of Secular Humanistic Jews, believe that survival of the

Jewish people depends on a broad view of Jewish identity. We welcome into the Jewish people all men and women who sincerely desire to share the Jewish experience regardless of their ancestry. We challenge the assumption that the Jews are primarily or exclusively a religious community and that religious convictions or behaviour are essential to full membership in the Jewish people.

The Jewish people is a world with a pluralistic culture and civilization all its own. Judaism, as the culture of the Jews, is more than theological commitment. It encompasses many languages, a vast body of literature, historical memories and ethical values. In our times the shadow of the Holocaust and the rebirth of the State of Israel are a central part of Jewish consciousness.

We Jews have a moral responsibility to welcome all people who seek to identify with our culture and destiny. The children and spouses of inter-marriage who desire to be part of the Jewish people must not be cast aside because they do not have Jewish mothers and do not wish to undergo religious conversion. The authority to define 'who is a Jew' belongs to all the Jewish people and cannot be usurped by any part of it.

In response to the destructive definition of a Jew now proclaimed by some Orthodox authorities, and in the name of the historic experience of the Jewish people, we therefore, affirm that a Jew is a person of Jewish descent or any person who declares himself or herself to be a Jew and who identifies with the history, ethical values, culture, civilization, community and fate of the Jewish people.[2]

Such an ideology of Judaism is based on a radical reinterpretation of the tradition. In *Judaism Beyond God*, Sherwin Wine offered a critique of the different religious movements within the Jewish community. Modern Orthodoxy, Conservatism, Reconstructionism and Reform are, in his view, the 'ambivalents'. Although these groups endorse the secular revolution in their everyday activities, they have one foot in the world of faith and the other in that of reason. However, since these two spheres are incompatible, such a stance is incoherent. Ambivalents, Wine asserted, are experts in avoiding actuality – they seek to avoid any form of painful confrontation. Unable to disown either faith or reason, they attempt to combine the humility of prayer with the dignity of personal freedom.

For Wine modern Orthodoxy avoids facing crucial dilemmas concerning belief in the Messiah, divine reward and punishment, and the World-to-Come. In place of theological commitment, Orthodox Judaism has substituted rigid adherence to traditional observance. Yet, without the religious basis of the faith, there is little reason to follow Jewish law. The Conservative movement has similarly failed to confront the challenges of modern secularism and as a result is riddled with theological inconsistency. Reconstructionism differs from Conservative Judaism in its rejection of belief in God; nonetheless, Reconstructionist Jews continue to use the religious vocabulary of the Jewish past. This has resulted in general confusion about the tenets of the faith. Reform Judaism, too, suffers from numerous defects. In particular its emphasis on ethical monotheism is, to Wine, a betrayal of modern secular culture and the Jewish heritage.

Humanistic Judaism, however, rejects the authority of the rabbinic tradition; it is also distinct from Conservative, Reform and Reconstructionist Judaism in jettisoning theistic language. Such a shift in perspective is due to the influence of science, capitalism and secular culture which have dramatically transformed Jewish life. As proponents of a secular Jewish lifestyle, Humanistic Jews believe in the power and beauty of human potential, the necessity of reason, the right of each person to satisfy his needs, and the goal of the unity of humankind. In this quest, Humanistic Judaism aspires to create a better future.

Such a modernized vision of Judaism is based on a number of assumptions concerning the central elements of the faith, as described in detail in the official *Guide to Humanistic Judaism* produced by the movement.

GOD

Historically belief in the existence of God served as the foundation of the Jewish tradition. After the Enlightenment, however, a growing number of Jews found it increasingly difficult to believe in an omnipotent, omniscient and benevolent creator and sustainer of the universe. Instead, a series of alternative theological positions has emerged within the community:

1.   **Theism:** Belief in a Supreme Being, a supernatural creator-God who responds to prayer and worship and intervenes actively in the lives of people.
2.   **Deism:** Belief in a Supreme Being, a supernatural creator who does not intervene in the lives of people.
3.   **Pantheism:** Belief that God and nature are one and the same, or that God and some part of nature, such as life, are one and the same.
4.   **Agnosticism:** Not knowing whether or not a Supreme Being exists.
5.   **Atheism:** Belief that a Supreme Being does not exist.
6   **Ignosticism:** Finding the question of God's existence meaningless because it has no verifiable consequences.

Unlike the other branches of Judaism, Humanistic Judaism denies any form of supernatural belief. Instead it is compatible with agnosticism, atheism and ignosticism. As such, it regards religious belief as fundamentally psychological in origin.

REVELATION

Unlike Orthodox Judaism which is based on the doctrine of *Torah MiSinai*, Humanistic Jews rely on reason as the most effective means of arriving at truth. Both scripture and rabbinic sources are perceived as human in origin; thus they must be submitted to critical evaluation. Viewed in this light, the *Torah* is regarded as an unreliable guide to the history of the Jewish people – Humanistic Jews believe it is full of misunderstanding and confusion. Nor is the *Torah* considered a viable ethical guide. Yet, Humanistic Jews can derive a number of important moral principles from scripture. Some of the Bible's ethical teaching is valid from a Humanistic outlook.

THE JEWISH PEOPLE

A central principle of rabbinic Judaism is that the Jewish nation was elected by God to be his special people, the instrument for the enlightenment of all humanity. In return for having been divinely elected, the Jewish community is bound to serve God by obeying his laws as found in the *Torah* and *Talmud* – the covenant between the deity and the people of Israel is fundamental to the faith. Humanistic Judaism, however, views all human beings as equal. Their differing worldviews are simply the result of historical, social and cultural factors; as a consequence, it is a mistake to view one group as superior to any other.

Adopting a secular perspective, Humanistic Jews reject the traditional interpretation of Jewish history – the account of the Jews in the Bible and rabbinic literature is seen as a blend of historical fact and mythic fantasy. The true history of the Jewish nation, however, is in the process of being discovered through the findings of biblical criticism, archaeology and scientific investigation.

In this light Humanistic Judaism is able to uncover events of Humanistic import in the Jewish past. Humanistic Judaism then – unlike Orthodox, Conservative and Reform Judaism – stresses that Jewish history is ultimately a human construction. Whereas these other branches of Judaism look to God's providential concern, Humanistic Jews see only universal indifference. Secular Humanistic Judaism offers a non-theistic alternative to Jewish identity and culture, promoting values that have been largely neglected by the Jewish establishment: rationality, personal autonomy and the celebration of human values. As a movement, it seeks to create a pluralistic world among all religions and philosophies of life.

For Humanistic Jews the Jewish holidays are of historical and religious significance in so far as they promote Humanistic values. Thus the sabbath is viewed as a day of peace, restoration and study. Above all it is a time to affirm and celebrate Jewish identity. Following traditional practice, Humanistic Jews are encouraged to observe home and community ceremonies:

> Shabbat offers opportunities for both home and community ceremonies: candlelighting, wine and the eating of braided bread (hallah), with blessings that express human power and responsibility. Shabbat celebrations for Humanistic Jews are tributes to Jewish solidarity, to the shared Jewish past, present, and future. They provide opportunities to learn about, articulate, discuss and celebrate Humanistic and Jewish history, philosophy, and values. Humanistic Shabbat celebrations recognize the individual's

connections to humanity: a family, a community, a nation, the world.[3]

Similarly, the *Havdalah* ceremony at the conclusion of the sabbath has important Humanistic implications:

> The symbols of the Havdalah – the twisted candle, the spices, and the wine – may be used Humanistically. The twisted candle represents the many sources of the light of wisdom and beauty. Wine symbolizes joy and fulfilment. The sweet, lingering fragrance of the spice box recalls all that is good and beautiful, and offers hope for happiness and peace in the coming week.[4]

Like the adherents of the other branches of contemporary Judaism, Humanistic Jews also view the New Year as spiritually significant – it is a time for reflection, renewal and new beginnings. Humanistic Judaism, however, focuses on the role of self-evaluation rather than divine judgment: *Rosh Hashanah* offers an occasion for Humanistic Jews to consider the possibilities for self-improvement. In this context the sounding of the *shofar* is perceived as summoning the Humanistic community to reflect on their personal shortcomings and to uphold Humanistic values. In a similar vein, the Day of Atonement is seen as signalling the climax of such self-evaluation – it affords an opportunity to make amends and seek forgiveness.

The three pilgrim festivals – Passover, *Sukkot* and *Shavuot* – also have important significance for Humanistic Jews. Although Jewish Humanism rejects the theological assumptions of the exodus account, Passover teaches the valuable lesson of liberation: it extols the quest for freedom in a variety of readings commemorating this pivotal event in the history of the nation. Like Passover, *Sukkot* was celebrated in ancient times as a major pilgrim festival; it is a reminder of the exodus from Egypt when Jews were commanded to construct booths and dwell in them. For Humanistic Jews, *Sukkot* symbolizes human mastery of the environment. *Shavuot*, the third pilgrim festival, marks the beginning of Jewish literature; it is understood as a time to celebrate the study of Jewish sources.

Like the other branches of contemporary Judaism, Jewish Humanism has also embraced a variety of ceremonies dealing with birth, puberty, marriage and death. Yet unlike the Jewish holidays, these events are perceived as having universal significance – in each case, commemorations associated with each stage point beyond the Jewish community to all humankind. Such a reinterpretation of the faith constitutes a decisive departure from the Jewish past. For those unable to subscribe to a belief in a supernatural deity but who nonetheless desire to identify themselves as Jews, Humanistic Judaism offers a new and radical approach to the Jewish way of life. We can see therefore that traditional Jewish existence is under severe attack. For a growing number of Jews, belief in God has given way to a sentimental attachment to Jewish folkways and a commitment to the continuing survival of a non-supernatural form of the Jewish faith.

JEWISH ASSIMILATION

As we have seen, the Jewish community has fragmented into a variety of religious groups each with its own ideology and interpretation of the Jewish heritage. Traditional Judaism has thus ceased to bind the community into a homogeneous entity. In addition, traditional values have been undermined by those outside these movements who have removed themselves from the Jewish community.

UNAFFILIATED JEWS

In our study of the American Jewish community in *The American Jew*, my wife and I frequently encountered individuals who had totally disassociated themselves from Judaism – some of these persons simply assimilated into the secular world. As one of these assimilated Jews told us, he married a non-Jew and through the years had no particular affinity with the tradition:

> I've never belonged to a synagogue in Metropolis. As a matter of fact, it's fair to say I've never really thought about the question. Beth and I were a unit.

We lived in a world which had frequent contact with both the Jewish and non-Jewish world. We didn't have children. How would I have brought them up? You're asking me a hypothetical question that I don't know that I can answer. I think probably as agnostics and with the moral virtues, and that's it! I would say I am not religious. I was not particularly interested in Jewish religion, even in Jewish history. I don't even recall any religious discussions. Did I think of myself as a Jew? No ... that was not my uppermost thought and reaction ... Over the years, I may have become slightly more sensitive to being a Jew, but it is not my first consideration in meeting people or in doing things. In fact it's way down the list.[1]

Some of the unaffiliated Jews we met lost interest in Judaism because they were unable to accept the religious principles of the faith; for these Jews, Jewish beliefs were totally implausible. An individual from an Orthodox background explained his early disillusionment with the Jewish tradition:

I could not reconcile anything these people were talking about with anything that made any sense: miracles, prohibitions – keep the whole thing! I used to go to the Metropolis Science Museum. The folks took me; I went there all the time. I loved it. You see these prehistoric things, and all that stuff. When I learned how to read, I see these things are sixty million years old. They got dates on em. How come then, in religion school, the calendar is 5,000 and some years old? So I start thinking about it. This was when I was probably seven or eight. And I say, 'There's something wrong here. These people are telling me the world started 5,000 years ago and these things are sixty million years old.' So I go into the rabbi and I say, 'How come?' He says, 'That's the way it is.' And I say, 'How can you say that's the way it is? I'm reading the Bible already, and I don't see anything about dinosaurs in there. Somewhere, somebody's got something wrong. I don't know who, but somebody's got something wrong.' And all he keeps telling me is, 'That is what we believe in. Believe in it.' I say, 'Thank you', and out I go. Screw you and your whole deal![2]

A Holocaust survivor who had been brought up in a secular household told us that beauty had taken the place of religious commitment:

I cannot tell you that I particularly believed in God. I believed so strongly in my parents that they took on the role of authority. In my reliance on them, I did not ever have the desire to believe in something besides us. The authority and the meaningfulness was really taking place within our household. Belief or non-belief in God never came up. We did not take much notice of religious holidays except that we were taken out of school, which was very nice! ... Beauty has been my passion. Music was what connected me with my parents, and my experience is that when it is beautiful, it is uplifting. I travel a lot for opera, and it is uplifting to me as an experience.[3]

Because aesthetics play such a fundamental role in this person's life, she and her husband decided that at their deaths sculpture and music would take the place of a formal religious observance:

> We know that we wanted to be cremated. We don't want a tombstone, but we commissioned this piece of sculpture carved by a husband and wife team. It's a large book made of Florentine marble. It's warped and it represents age. When one of us dies, the other one will pay for a quartet to play in the house. There will be good food, good drink and good music. People can talk about the departed one. The ashes will be put in pots which I've already commissioned and these will be buried in the cemetery and the book will go on top.[4]

Other Jews have found it increasingly difficult to identify with the Jewish community because they have inter-married. In one instance, the person we spoke to had also adopted an Oriental child. Although this individual regarded herself as Jewish, she and her husband did not wish to identify with the Jewish community and sought to raise their child as a secular humanist:

> I want her to grow up as a secular American humanist. I want her to care about other people, to have a sense of responsibility for her community, and to take pride in herself and her varied background. I do not particularly want her to have a Jewish education. I don't think I will send her to religion school.[5]

The growth of intermarried couples has had a profound effect on Jewish identity. A number of Jewish institutions have attempted to integrate these couples and their children, but this has proved difficult in many cases. Often the non-Jewish partner is perplexed as to how to integrate his family into a Jewish setting. Thus a non-Jewish spouse told us of his confusion:

> A few years ago, when the kids were six or so, we were thinking about how to give them a proper sense of values. So we sent them to the temple Shalom 'Every Day, the Jewish Way' programme. Tom went for one year. He had a scepticism which I share, so he dropped out. Barbara, my daughter, went for two years. She enjoyed it, but they both thought it too slow; they were a bit bored ... We go to the Presbyterian church about once a year to listen to the hymns. I have great affection for the Quakers, but at this point my politics and theirs differ. We made another stab at religious training. In the home, for a number of years, we lit Friday night candles. We have a Christmas tree and presents – they get both Hanukkah and Christmas presents! In past years, we've been through short forms of the Passover service. Easter eggs? Sometimes, yeah ... Would I want them to marry someone Jewish? The quality of person is more important to me than the religion.[6]

For a number of converts to Judaism, there is similarly a sense of unease about Jewish identity. One of the converts we interviewed spoke at length about her negative feelings towards the community:

> When we announced we were going to get married, the balloon went up ... His family insisted, absolutely insisted, on a Jewish wedding, and if we were to have a Jewish wedding, then I had to convert. There was no option ... to begin with, I went along with it. I wanted to please his folks. But it was a bummer from the start. I had an awful interview with the rabbi. Without exactly saying so, he made it quite clear he couldn't understand why a boy like Joe would want to get involved with a little tramp like me ... Anyway, I went along to the weekly conversion class. I had to ... Every week we had to go to the temple ... It was all so silly ... and so different from what I was used to ... Our kids ... we're not bringing them up in any religion. They can decide for themselves when they're old enough ... It was all a long time ago now. I wish I had something more positive to tell you.[7]

Such individuals, though formally part of the community, have fallen away from any form of Jewish practice. Others, too, have dropped out of Jewish life even though they are perceived as Jewish by the community because of their birth. Some of these Jews have sought spiritual enlightenment in other religions. One Jewish girl we talked to had been so disenchanted with the Judaism of her youth, that she became a Hare Krishna devotee. Movingly she explained her spiritual journey away from Judaism:

When did I check out of Judaism? I don't know. I don't think in that way. My mind and body will probably always be Jewish. There will always be a Jewish part of me. But I am a spirit-soul, and the knowledge of Bhakti has been very fulfilling. I feel my identity with this tradition predates my identity with Judaism. I felt it very strongly. It all clicked when I first went to India ... Personally I don't feel that God is going to mind if you worship Him by bowing down, or standing up, or calling Him one name or another. The point is to call God.[8]

Another person we interviewed had broken with Judaism and became a Roman Catholic. Yet, she too was conscious of her Jewish origins and still perceived herself as Jewish:

The second Christmas I was here I went to mass with some friends, and that night I decided it was time to become a Christian. I was living Christianity anyway. I started going to classes immediately in January, and I continued for over a year ... I'm much happier. I finally felt I belong. I always prayed to be part of a larger family, and I've got very involved with their church in all sorts of projects. Catholics want to get back to their roots. I always thought I had better hide my Judaism, but it's very special to the Church that I was a Jew — very precious. I'm asked to speak: I've conducted Passover *seders*; I've read the Old Testament in Hebrew.[9]

A very different approach to the Jewish heritage was expressed by a Jewish astrologer we met. As she explained, her early experience of Judaism was devoid of spirituality. Growing up in a Reform context, she found little to deepen her faith:

> You really want me to tell you what I learned at temple Shalom? I learnt that there is something morally wrong with chewing gum ... and that's about it ... What I got from temple Shalom was roughly the equivalent of spiritual bankruptcy. It was definitely not a positive experience. It was serving a jail sentence. What I learnt at religion school was about Jewish baseball. They were trying to secularize the religion.[10]

In place of established religion, this person turned to Jewish astrology to discover a source of spirituality:

> What astrology taught me is that we have a universe which is orderly and structured. Science is based on predictability as well ... in the Middle Ages Jews were the best astrologers. I also found that a lot of traditional Jewish superstitions are solidly grounded in metaphysical and astrological principles ... So suddenly, a great many of those superstitions made sense – when they made no sense at all in terms of enlightened reason ... Astrology is very much part of the Jewish tradition. The more I study, the more I realize that it is part of my birthright.[11]

The unaffiliated members of the Jewish community hence range across a broad spectrum of belief and practice. Yet, despite the differences in approach, they have all disassociated themselves from the formal established structures of the faith. These Jews who have distanced themselves from both traditional belief and practice illustrate the ways in which contemporary Jewry is radically different from Jews in the past. No longer is the community united by a common set of beliefs and practices in the face of a hostile world. Instead, modern Jews have assimilated and integrated into the societies in which they live, thereby losing any sense of a religious and cultural heritage.

Rejecting Judaism

Through the centuries, Jewry was united by a common heritage. As we have seen, the Jewish people subscribed to a belief in one God who created the cosmos, chose the Jews as his special people, and guides history to its ultimate fulfilment. In the unfolding of this scheme, the children of Israel have a major role – they are to be a light to the nations. In modern times, however, the Jewish community has fragmented into various religious groupings with their own religious orientations. The dissolution of traditional belief and practice has brought about radical changes in the nature of Jewish existence. In the view of traditionalists, this is the tragedy of the modern age.

Rejecting the Traditional Jewish Way of Life

In *Why Be Jewish?*, the late Orthodox activist Rabbi Meir Kahane castigated the contemporary Jewish community for its rejection of traditional Jewish values. 'The truth', he wrote, 'is that huge numbers of Jews simply find nothing of importance in the concept of being Jewish. It is, at best, irrelevant to them and, in a number of cases, distasteful to their view of life … It is the Jews who are for everything – but Judaism. Who struggle for political causes that are non-Jewish and, many times, anti-Jewish. It is the Jews who desperately need spiritual answers and who turn to Christianity or to Eastern Mysticism or to Satanism. It is those who turn to drugs and to alcohol and to every conceivable solution because they neither know nor care to know about their heritage.'[1]

What, he asks, is the meaning of the Jewish faith, if it is stripped of its religious foundation:

> Having destroyed the Divine origin of Judaism, what remains of the obligation to continue Judaism as an organized religion? If its uniqueness – the special, exclusive rituals and commandments – are indeed no longer Divine truth, then we may freely discard them and retain only the ethical or moral concepts. And, indeed, this is what Reform has done. But, of course, this is not the end. For if we are left here only with ethics, then how do we differ from other peoples and tongues and faiths?[2]

As we have seen, the disintegration of the traditional Jewish way of life occurred in the wake of the Enlightenment. After centuries of discrimination and persecution, Jews were free to assimilate and integrate into the societies in which they resided. Under the impact of modern science and contemporary secular trends, the monolithic system of Jewish belief and practice has undergone a process of dissolution. Regarding the concept of God, a number of Jewish thinkers have found it increasingly difficult to accept the fundamental tenets of the Jewish faith: some wish to modify various elements of Jewish theism, imposing limits to God's omnipotence or omniscience; others have sought a more radical solution, wishing to substitute the concept of a supernatural deity in naturalistic terms. As we noted, the Reconstructionist thinker Mordecai Kaplan asserted that the idea of God must be redefined – the belief in a supernatural deity must be superseded by a concept of God as 'man's will to live'. At the far end of the religious spectrum, an even more radical approach has been advanced by Humanistic Jews who wish to dispense with God altogether. For these Jews, it is possible to live a Jewishly religious life without any acknowledgement of a divine reality. Thus, across the various denominations in contemporary Judaism, there exists a wide range of different and conflicting beliefs about the nature of the divine – no longer is the Jewish community committed to the view that God created and sustains the universe, guiding it to its ultimate fulfilment.

Similarly, for many Jews the traditional belief in *Torah MiSinai* no longer seems plausible. The rabbinic understanding of *Torah* as revealed to Moses and infallibly transmitted through the sages has been undermined by the findings of modern scholarship. From the earliest period, reformers continued to believe in divine revelation, but they were anxious to point out that God's disclosure is mediated by human understanding. According to Reform Judaism, the Bible is a spiritual record of the history of ancient Israel, reflecting the primitive spiritual ideas of its own age. Similarly, the Conservative movement views scripture as historically conditioned and mediated through human apprehension. As the Conservative scholar Solomon Schechter explained, the *Torah* is not in heaven – it is on earth and must be interpreted to be understood. For Reconstructionist Jews, the *Torah* is a human document, shaped by those who composed this epic account of Israel's origins and development. In this light, the Reconstructionist movement seeks to incorporate the Bible into the life of its members without ascribing to it a supernatural origin. Humanistic Jews share a similar veneration of the *Torah* even though they do not believe it was divinely revealed. Hence, as in the case of beliefs about God, there are fundamental differences of opinion regarding the status of scripture among the various branches of contemporary Judaism.

The doctrine of messianic redemption has likewise been radically modified within the various branches of non-Orthodox Judaism. In the earliest stages of development, reformers rejected the notion of a personal Messiah; instead, they believed that the Messianic Age was beginning to dawn in their own time. In their view, history was evolving progressively towards an era of liberty, equality and justice for all people. Even though the events of the twentieth century have eclipsed these earlier messianic expectations, Reform Judaism still embraces the conviction that human progress is possible in the modern world. Similarly, many Zionists saw the foundation of a Jewish homeland as the fulfilment of messianic hope. Rejecting the belief in a personal

Messiah, they advocated a naturalistic interpretation of historical progress in which the Jewish people would be restored to the land of their ancestors. Such reinterpretations of traditional belief are indicative of the general shift away from supernaturalism in the modern world.

The doctrine of the resurrection of the dead has likewise been largely rejected in both the Orthodox and non-Orthodox camps. The original belief in resurrection was an eschatologial hope bound up with the rebirth of the nation in the Days of the Messiah, but as this messianic concept faded into the background so did this doctrine. For most Jews, physical resurrection is simply inconceivable in the light of the scientific understanding of the world. In the view of many Jewish thinkers, the doctrine of resurrection is unduly materialistic. In the Reform community, such a belief has been firmly rejected; in its place the concept of the immortality of the soul has been widely accepted.

The belief in eternal punishment has also been discarded by a large number of Jews partly because of the interest in penal reform during the past century. Punishment as retaliation in a vindictive sense has been generally rejected. As the Jewish scholar Louis Jacobs has remarked: 'the value of punishment as a deterrent and for the protection of society is widely recognized. Against such a background the whole question of reward and punishment in the theological sphere is approached in a more questioning spirit.'[3] Further, the rabbinic view of hell is seen by many as morally repugnant. Jewish theologians have stressed that it is a delusion to believe that a God of love could have created a place of eternal punishment.

Traditional theological belief has thus lost its force for a large number of Jews in modern society – no longer is it possible to discover a common core of religious belief underpinning Jewish life. The community instead is deeply divided on the most fundamental features of the Jewish tradition. Likewise, there is a parallel disunity within Jewry concerning Jewish observance. As far as Orthodoxy is concerned, it is in theory a system of law, going back consistently and without interruption for thousands of years to the beginning of Jewish history; all the elaborations of *halakhah* in the later Orthodox codes are held to be rediscoveries rather than novelties. Yet, this picture of an eternal developing legal system breaks down when we face its astonishing shrinkages in contemporary society – great areas of Jewish law have disappeared for a wide variety of reasons. Frequently, individuals who consider themselves Orthodox have simply ceased to resort to rabbinical courts in a number of areas of life. There is thus a large gap between the Orthodox system of practice and the limited observance of Jewish life within a large segment of the Orthodox Jewish community.

This rapidly contracting area of observance within Orthodoxy is in part the reason for the existence of Conservative Judaism. Since its inception, Conservative rabbis have been anxious to make Jewish law more flexible so as to provide for change legally. This approach to the tradition has provided a framework for the reinterpretation of Jewish law in the light of changed circumstances and modern needs. While acknowledging the historical importance of the Jewish heritage, the movement has sought to discover new ways to adjust the legal system where necessary. As a result, many traditional observances have been abandoned and other features altered to suit contemporary circumstances. In this way, Conservative Judaism has provided a means of legitimizing deviations from tradition, thereby contributing to the further shrinkage of the Jewish legal code.

Similarly, within Reform Judaism, there has been an attempt to reinterpret Jewish law in the light of contemporary conditions. As the Reform Jewish scholar Solomon Freehof explained:

> Some of its provisions have passed from our lives. We do not regret that fact. But as to those laws that we do follow, we wish them to be in harmony with tradition ... Our concern is more with people than with the legal system. Wherever possible, such interpretations are developed which are feasible and conforming to the needs of life. Sometimes, indeed, a request be answered in the negative when there is no way in the law for a permissive answer to be given. Generally the law is searched for such opinion as can conform with the realities of life.[4]

Due to such a liberal approach to the tradition, even greater areas of the legal system have been rejected within the ranks of Reform Judaism. For many Reform Jews, traditional Jewish law has no bearing on their everyday lives.

In contemporary society, therefore, there is a wide divergence concerning Jewish observances and ceremonies. At the far right, ultra-Orthodox Jews scrupulously adhere to the tradition, yet within the Orthodox camp there are many who have ignored the dictates of Jewish law. Within Conservative Judaism deviation from the *halakhah* is legitimized, resulting in the abandonment of large areas of the tradition. And on the left, within Reform and Humanistic Judaism, there is virtual abandonment of the traditional *Code of Jewish Law*. Hence, within the Jewish community there is no agreement about either practice or religious belief: the monolithic character of traditional Judaism as it existed from ancient times to the Enlightenment has been replaced by chaos and confusion across the religious spectrum. Jews disagree today as to the fundamentals of the faith and the place of Judaism in their lives.

PART II

ANTI-SEMITISM AND
JEWISH RENEWAL

BIBLICAL JUDAISM AND THE DIASPORA

The story of Jewish suffering opens with the Hebrew scriptures, which record the history of anti-Jewish sentiment beginning with the events of the exodus. As the centuries passed, the Jewish nation endured repeated calamities: in Hellenistic times antipathy towards Jews and Judaism was fiercely expressed by both political leaders and authors; such animosity continued throughout the Greco-Roman period and was crystallized in the writings of prominent figures of the age. Yet despite such hostility, the Jewish people remained loyal to the Jewish heritage. Through the exodus, the Jewish people forged their religious identity in the wilderness, conquered the land of Canaan, built the temple, and became a nation. Eventually when the Romans vanquished the Jews and destroyed Jerusalem, the Jewish people recreated themselves in the diaspora. Ancient Jew-hatred thus repeatedly led to the revitalization of the Jewish nation and their determination to remain loyal to the traditions of their ancestors.

EXODUS AND LIBERATION

The Hebrew Bible recounts the earliest known instance of hostility to the Jews in Pharaoh's persecution of the Jewish population prior to the exodus. According to the book of Exodus, Pharaoh expressed concern at the growing numbers and potential disloyalty of the Jewish population living in Egypt:

> Now there arose a new king over Egypt, who did not know Joseph. And he said to his people, 'Behold the people of Israel are too many and too mighty for us. Come let us deal shrewdly with them, lest they multiply, and if war befall us, they join their enemies and fight against us and escape from the land.' (Exod. 1:8–10)

Even though the Egyptians mistrusted the Jews, the Jewish community grew in strength, which caused dread among the Egyptians. Eventually Pharaoh resolved to kill all firstborn sons. Speaking to the Hebrew midwives, he declared:

> When you serve as midwives to the Hebrew women, and seat them upon the birthstool, if it is a son, you shall kill him; but if it is a daughter, she shall live. (Exod. 1:16)

However, the midwives feared God's wrath and did not comply, allowing the male children to live. As a consequence, the Pharaoh condemned all the people:

> Every son that is born to the Hebrews you shall cast
> into the Nile, but you shall let every daughter live.
> (Exod. 1:22)

Here the motive for such contempt was not racial
prejudice, economic envy or disdain for Jewish ways:
rather scripture states that the Pharaoh acted out of fear
for his own nation.

The biblical narrative continues with an account of
the deliverance of the Jews from Egyptian bondage. The
book of Exodus relates that a son had been born to Amram
of the house of Levi and his wife Jochebed. When he was
three months old, his parents concealed him among the
reeds growing on the banks of the Nile to save him from
Pharaoh's decree. Pharaoh's daughter found the child and
adopted him as her son, Moses. When he became older,
he attacked and killed a taskmaster who was oppressing a
Hebrew slave, and fled to the desert. Here he dwelt with
Jethro (a priest of Midian) and married his daughter,
Zipporah. Eventually God revealed himself to Moses
out of a burning bush, commanding that he deliver the
chosen people from Pharaoh's harsh bondage:

> I am the God of your father, the God of Abraham,
> the God of Isaac, and the God of Jacob ... I have
> seen the affliction of my people who are in Egypt,
> and have heard their cry because of their taskmasters;
> I know their sufferings ... Come, I will send you to
> Pharaoh that you may bring forth my people, the sons
> of Israel, out of Egypt. (Exod. 3:6–7, 10)

To persuade Pharaoh that he should let the Jewish people go, God inflicted a series of plagues on the Egyptians (blood, frogs, lice, flies, pestilence, skin disease, hail, locusts, darkness) culminating in the slaying of every Egyptian firstborn son. The firstborn of the Israelites were spared as each family slaughtered a lamb and smeared its blood on the doorposts. Seeing this, the Angel of Death passed over the household. After this final plague, Pharaoh released the Israelites, and they fled without even waiting for their bread to rise. However, the perils were not over; Pharaoh changed his mind and sent his forces in pursuit. When the Israelites came to an expanse of water, it seemed they were trapped. Miraculously it was converted to dry land by a strong wind so that they were able to escape. The Egyptians, however, were drowned as they chased after them:

> The Egyptians pursued, and went in after them into the midst of the sea, all Pharaoh's horses, his chariots, and his horsemen ... The waters returned and covered the chariots and the horsemen and all the host of Pharaoh that had followed them into the sea; not so much as one of them remained. (Exod. 14:23, 28)

When the Israelites witnessed this event, they sang a song to God:

> I will sing to the Lord, for he has triumphed gloriously;
> the horse and his rider he has thrown into the sea.
> The Lord is my strength and my song,

and he has become my salvation;
this is my God, and I will praise him,
my father's God, and I will exalt him.
The Lord is a man of war;
the Lord is his name. (Exod. 15:1–3)

When the Pharaoh's horses and his chariots and his horsemen went into the sea, the Lord brought back the waters of the sea upon them, but the Israelites crossed on dry land. Then Miriam, the prophetess, the sister of Aaron, took the timbrel in her hand, and all the women went out after her with timbrels and dancing and Miriam sang:

Sing unto the Lord, for he has triumphed gloriously;
the horse and his rider he has thrown into the sea.
(Exod. 15:21)

Even though it is impossible to know whether the exodus ever took place, the narrative has served as a central orienting event in the life and thought of the Jewish people throughout its history. The Passover *seder* envisages the exodus experience as a symbol of freedom from oppression, and the whole of the *Haggadah* is pervaded by the image of God as the saviour of humankind. For this reason the Passover service begins with the ancient formulaic invitation to those who hunger or are in need to participate in the festival:

This is the bread of affliction that our fathers ate in the Land of Egypt. All who hunger, let them come and eat: all who are in need, let them come and celebrate the Passover. Now we are here – next year we shall be free men.

Any Jew who sits down to the Passover meal and is oblivious to the call of those who are in want has missed the meaning of the celebration.

During the service the leader displays the unleavened bread to stimulate the curiosity of the youngsters at the meal. It is then the turn of the youngest child to ask about the nature of the Passover festivities. The entire ritual of the *seder* hinges on these enquiries. In reply the leader recites the narrative of the exodus, stressing the themes of liberation and freedom from oppression:

We were Pharaoh's henchmen in Egypt; and the Lord our God brought us out thereof with a mighty hand and an outstretched arm. Now, had not the Holy One brought our fathers from Egypt, then we and our children and our children's children would be enslaved to Pharaoh in Egypt. Wherefore, even were we all wise men, all men of understanding, all advanced in years, all men with knowledge of the *Torah*, it would yet be our duty to recount the story of the coming forth from Egypt; and all who recount at length the story of the coming forth from Egypt are verily to be praised.

This response implies that the Passover does not simply commemorate a triumph of remote antiquity. Rather, the Passover ceremony is a celebration of the emancipation of each Jew in every generation, for had it not been for the exodus Jews would still be slaves in Egypt.

The keynote of the *Haggadah* is enshrined in a central pledge of the *seder*:

> It is this Divine pledge that hath stood by our fathers and by us also. Not only one man hath risen against us to destroy us, but in every generation men have risen against us to destroy us: But the Holy One delivereth us always from their hand.

Here Pharaoh's action is seen as a paradigm of all attempts by Israel's enemies to persecute the Jewish people. Echoes of centuries of persecution are evoked by these words, yet it is made clear that God has been, and will continue to be, on the side of oppressed people. In the symbols of the Passover meal, deliverance is re-enacted. Explaining this symbolism the leader states with regard to the shankbone of the lamb:

> The Passover Lamb that our fathers used to eat when the temple was still standing – that was because the Holy One, Blessed be He, passed over the house of our fathers in Egypt, as it is said: 'Ye shall say, It is the sacrifice of the Lord's Passover, who passed over the houses of the children of Israel in Egypt, when He smote the Egyptians and delivered our houses.' And the people bowed the head and worshipped.

The unleavened bread is the bread of affliction, the historical emblem of the exodus. The leader declares that it is the symbol of sympathy for the enslaved as well as that of freedom from oppression:

> This unleavened bread that we eat – what is the reason? It is because there was no time for our ancestors' dough to become leavened, before the King, King of all Kings, the Holy One, revealed Himself to them and redeemed them, as it is said: 'And they baked unleavened cakes of the dough which they brought forth out of Egypt, for it was not leavened: because they were thrust out of Egypt, and could not tarry, neither had they prepared for themselves any victual.'

The bitter herbs, the symbol of bitterness and servitude, remind the Jews that it is their duty as descendants of slaves to lighten the stranger's burden:

> This bitter herb that we eat – what is its reason? It is because the Egyptians embittered the life of our ancestors in Egypt, as it is said: 'And they made their lives bitter with hard bondage, in mortar and brick, and in all manner of service in the field, all their service, when they made them serve, was with rigour.'

The lesson of the Passover service, deeply engraved on the hearts of the Jewish nation, is that persecution and divine deliverance are realities of the present as well as the past. In each generation, Jews must think of themselves as delivered from a perpetual enemy and should assume responsibility for rescuing those who suffer under oppression.

The exodus narrative thus constitutes a paradigm of victory over oppression. The Passover celebration which commemorates this event is a symbolic exaltation of freedom: Jews are all to rejoice in the liberation of their ancestors. Throughout the history of the Jewish people this festival has awakened the spirit of the people to the significance of human liberation. The biblical account of the exodus – embodied in the liturgy of the *Haggadah* – has played a central role in the quest for human dignity and freedom and has shaped Jewish consciousness through the ages. Jew-hatred therefore served to unite the Jewish nation and led to the fulfilment of God's promise to Abraham that they would settle in the land of Cannan. Out of despair the Jewish people prospered and flourished, and saw in their liberation a source of hope and inspiration, even during the darkest hours of Jewish history.

TRIUMPH AND DESPAIR

Once the Jewish people settled in the promised land, they were ruled over by the judges. Later when the country divided into the kingdom of Israel in the north and the kingdom of Judah in the south, the people were subject to a series of kings. In the eighth century BCE, however, the Assyrians conquered the country. This was followed two centuries later by a Babylonian assault on the southern kingdom in 586 BCE. Jerusalem was devastated, the temple destroyed, and the Israelites led into captivity. Nonetheless the nation revived despite such devastation.

TRAGEDY AND REVIVAL

The book of Lamentations records the tragedy of exile:

> How lonely sits the city
> that was full of people!
> How like a widow has she become,
> she that was great among the nations! ...
> The roads to Zion mourn,
> for none come to the appointed feasts;
> all her gates are desolate,
> her priests groan. (Lamentations 1:1, 4)

Yet, the ancient Israelites did not despair. The post-exilic prophets proclaimed that God had not forsaken his people, and that eventually they would be restored to their ancient land. Second Isaiah, for example, sought to comfort the nation:

> Comfort, comfort my people,
> says your God.
> Speak tenderly to Jerusalem,
> and cry to her
> that her warfare is ended,
> that her iniquity is pardoned,
> that she has received from the Lord's hand
> double for all her sins. (Isaiah 40:1–2)

According to the prophet, the Lord will return in triumph to Jerusalem. He will act as a shepherd leading his flock: 'He will feed his flock like a shepherd, he will gather the lambs in his arms, he will carry them in his bosom, and gently lead those that are with young' (Isaiah 40:11). All the world will see this act of deliverance and acknowledge that there is no redeemer except for the Lord of Israel.

By the end of the sixth century, Cyrus the Great who had conquered the Babylonians decreed that the Jews should return to Judah and rebuild the temple. In his edict, he declared:

> The Lord, the God of heaven, has given me all the kingdoms of the earth, and he has charged me to build him a house at Jerusalem, which is in Judah. Whoever is among you of all his people, may his God

> be with him, and let him go up to Jerusalem, which
> is in Judah, and rebuild the house of the Lord, the
> God of Israel – he is the God who is in Jerusalem;
> and let each survivor, in whatever place he sojourns,
> be assisted by the men of his place with silver and
> gold, with goods and with beasts, besides freewill
> offerings for the house of God which is in Jerusalem.
> (Ezra 1.2–4).

In response to this edict, the leaders of the Jewish
nation made extensive preparations for this journey. The
returning exiles were given vessels of silver and gold as
well as goods and beasts, and Cyrus also brought out
the vessels of the temple which Nebuchadnezzar had
carried away from Jerusalem. Hence, out of tragedy the
Jewish nation was renewed, the temple was rebuilt, and
Jerusalem restored.

The theme of victory over despair is also a central
theme of the festival of *Purim* which commemorates the
victory of the Jewish nation over its enemies during the
Second Temple period. The book of Esther deals with
the Jewish community in the town of Susa, the Persian
capital during the reign of King Xerxes in the fifth
century BCE. According to some scholars, the book was
written in the second century BCE; other scholars date it
much earlier because of the number of Persian loan words
contained in the text as well as its oriental atmosphere. In
any event, the book no doubt reflects attitudes towards
the Jews during the period of the Second Temple.

The book opens by setting the scene – here the
grandeur of King Ahasurerus is depicted. In the third

year of his reign, he gave a banquet which lasted for 180 days. When Queen Vashti was ordered to appear before the people, she refused. The king was incensed and his advisers were concerned that Vashti's action would encourage other women to treat their husbands with contempt. At their urging, the king resolved to replace Vashti as queen. The king's attendants advised him to gather all the beautiful young virgins to his harem in Susa so that he could choose a suitable substitute.

When Esther – the niece of a Jew living in Susa – was chosen, she became the king's favourite. Subsequently her uncle Mordecai discovered a plot to overthrow the king which he revealed to Esther; Esther then told this to the king and the men who were guilty of treason were hanged. At this time the king promoted Haman as chief adviser and all except Mordecai bowed down to him. When Haman learned that Mordecai disobeyed the command to pay him homage, he was furious and sought to destroy all the Jews in the kingdom. The king gave his consent to Haman's scheme, and his secretaries were summoned to issue an edict giving orders to kill all Jews and confiscate their possessions. When Mordecai heard this edict, he appealed to Esther who pleaded on behalf of her people. Eventually, however, Haman was hanged on the gallows he had constructed for Mordecai.

These events are celebrated during the festival of *Purim* which, like Passover, commemorates the victory of the Jewish people over those who seek to destroy them. In most congregations *Purim* resembles a carnival – children frequently attend the reading from the scroll of Esther in fancy dress, and whenever Haman's name is mentioned, worshippers tap their feet and whirl noisemakers. In the *Amidah* and grace after meals a prayer of thanksgiving is included. During the afternoon a special festival meal takes place including such traditional dishes as *hamen-tashen*. On *Purim* it is customary to stage plays connected with this event. In mythological terms Haman personifies all of Israel's enemies through the ages who have sought the destruction of the Jewish nation. As in the case of the exodus, the theme of suffering and triumph is paramount.

During the reign of the Seleucids in the second century, two families engaged as rivals in the Judean Jewish community: the Tobiads and the Oniads. When Seleucus IV was murdered in 175 BCE and succeeded by Antiochus IV Epiphanes, Jason, a member of the Oniad family, bribed Antiochus IV to make him high priest in place of his brother Onias. When he was appointed to this position, Jason attempted to Hellenize Jerusalem. This involved the introduction of Greek games in which the athletes competed naked, a sight shocking to traditional religious sensibilities. Most Jews found these changes abhorrent, and Jason was deposed from the throne and replaced by Menelaus, a member of the Tobiad family.

While this internal conflict took place in Judea, Antiochus IV advanced against Egypt and defeated the Egyptian king, Ptolemy VI; on his return he robbed the Jerusalem temple. In 168 BCE Antiochus IV again invaded Egypt, but this time he encountered the Romans, who drove back his onslaught. In Jerusalem it was rumoured that Antiochus IV had been killed, and Jason quickly tried to remove Menelaus. Antiochus IV however acted speedily to crush this rebellion. He conquered Jerusalem and led off some of the people as slaves. In addition he banned circumcision, sabbath observance, and the reading of the *Torah*. He also decreed that the temple should be dedicated to the worship of the Greek god Zeus, that pigs should be sacrificed on the altar, and that all people, including non-Jews, should be allowed to worship there. Hellenism, which previously was encouraged by the Seleucids, thus became official policy.

Antiochus IV underestimated Jewish resistance to his reforms. Many Jews were prepared to die rather than violate their traditions. Eventually a guerrilla band, led by a priest Mattathias and his five sons, engaged in armed revolt. After Mattathias' death, this movement was spearheaded by his son Judas. Some Jews – the Hasideans – were opposed to armed struggle and retreated into the Judean desert where they were slaughtered by the Seleucids when they refused to fight in battle on the sabbath. The event drew other Jews to the side of the rebels, and after a series of military engagements the oppressive policies of the Seleucids were reversed. Jewish law was reinstituted, and the temple was restored and rededicated on 14 December 164 BCE, an event subsequently commemorated by the festival of *Hanukkah*.

The festival itself means dedication and is celebrated for eight days beginning on 25th of *Kislev* – it commemorates the victory of the Maccabees. The central observance of this festival is the kindling of the festive lamp on each of the eight nights. In ancient times this lamp was placed in the doorway or in the street outside; subsequently the lamp was placed inside the house. The lighting occurs after dark. The procedure for lighting the *Hanukkah* candles is to light one candle on the first night, and an additional candle each night until the last night when all eight candles are lit.

After kindling the first light, the following prayer is recited:

> We kindle these lights on account of the miracles, the deliverances and the wonders which thou didst work for our fathers, by means of the holy priests. During all the eight days of Hanukkah these lights are sacred, neither is it permitted us to make any profane use of them; but we are only to look at them, in order that we may give thanks unto thy name for thy miracles, thy deliverances and thy wonders.

In the home this hymn is chanted, recalling the victory of the ancient Israelites over the Egyptians, the restoration of the Jews from Babylonian exile, as well as the triumph over Haman:

> O Fortress, Rock of my salvation, unto thee it is becoming to give praise: let my house of prayer be restored, and I will there offer thee thanks-givings; when thou shalt have utterly destroyed the blaspheming foe, I will complete with song and psalm the dedication of the altar.

> Full sated was my soul with ills, my strength was spent with sorrow; they embittered my life by hardship

during my subjection to the domination of Egypt, but God with his great power brought forth the chosen race, while the host of Pharaoh and all his seed sank like a stone into the deep.

To his holy temple he brought me, yet there also I found no peace, for the oppressor came and led me captive, because I had served strange gods: I had to quaff the wine of bewilderment: well nigh had I perished when Babylon's end drew near; through Zerubbabel I was saved after seventy years.

The Agagite [Haman] the son of Hammedatha, sought to cut down the fir tree [Mordecai]; but this design became a snare to himself, and his pride was brought to an end. The head of the Benjamanite thou didst exalt, but the enemy's name thou didst blot out; the many sons he had gotten thou didst hang upon the gallows.

The Grecians were gathered against me in the days of the Hasmoneans; they broke down the walls of my towers, and defiled all the oils; but from one of the last remaining flasks a miracle was wrought for thy beloved, and their men of understanding appointed these eight days for song and praises.

With the consolidation of Hellenistic culture, Jews were increasingly perceived as alien. Distancing themselves from the majority population, they viewed Jerusalem as their holy city, and regarded the invisible God of scripture as the lord of the universe. Setting themselves apart, they perceived their host countries as profane and their fellow citizens as religiously blind. Living in a self-imposed ghetto, they segregated themselves from the rest of society. Such attitudes provoked resentment and fear, giving rise to venomous depictions of Jews and their religion. Yet such Judeophobia did not overwhelm Jewry. Instead the Jewish people triumphed over their enemies, and their victory is celebrated in myth and legend.

13

Destruction of the Temple and Rebirth

Under Roman rule, the Jewish population was subject to various forms of humiliation – this evoked intense anti-Roman feeling. Eventually such hostility led to war only to be followed by defeat and destruction of the Jerusalem temple. In 70 CE thousands of Jews were deported. Yet despite such defeat, the Pharisees carried on the Jewish tradition through teaching and study. Initially the rabbinic academy at Javneh near Jerusalem was the focus of Jewish learning. In time this centre of rabbinic scholarship was replaced by the great Babylonian academies. In these schools sages and scholars expounded the *Mishnah* and later codified the *Talmud* which was to become the central religious text of Jewish life for all time.

THE WAR AGAINST ROME AND RABBINIC JUDAISM

Under the Romans, the Jewish population in Judah was subject to various forms of humiliation. When the Romans instituted a census of the population, they provoked Jewish resentment since census-taking was contrary to Jewish law. Under the leadership of Judas the Galilean, a resistance movement (known as the Zealots) became active. Later the prefect Pontius Pilate experienced a number of difficulties with the Jewish community. They regarded his military standards bearing medallions of the emperor as idolatrous. Following demonstrations in Jerusalem, protesters encamped in front of Pilate's official residence at Caesarea Maritima and then in the stadium. Pilate also caused considerable consternation when he used a Jewish religious fund to pay for an aqueduct, and again when he set up gilded shields inscribed with both his and the emperor's names in the former palace of Herod.

Under Tiberus' nephew and successor Caligula, the Jews in Alexandria became embroiled in a conflict with the Roman authorities. These Jews had put forward a claim for full citizenship rights, thereby evoking a violent reaction from the Gentile Greek community. Mobs broke into synagogues and set up statues of the emperor. The Roman governor of Egypt ordered 38 members of the Jewish council to be flogged in the theatre while Jewish women were forced to eat pork. Caligula himself regarded the Jews' failure to recognize his divinity as lunacy. Meanwhile, at Javneh on the coast of Judea, the Greek community erected an altar in honour of Caligula. The Jewish community of Jamnia regarded this act as a deliberate provocation and destroyed it.

As a consequence, the emperor and his advisers decided to revive the policy of Antiochus IV Epiphanes; the temple and all synagogues were to be transformed into shrines of the imperial cult. Orders were given to the governor of Syria to construct a large statue of Caligula in the guise of Jupiter to be set up in Jerusalem. Two decades of procurators after the death of Agrippa in 44 CE marked a period of constant friction between Roman rulers and the Jewish population. When the Roman military presence was driven out by Jewish rebels, Vespasian, acting under the emperor Nero's orders, assembled an army in 67 CE. Although the fortress of Jotapata held out for 47 days, it eventually fell and the Romans slaughtered most of the population.

During the winter of 67–68 CE the Zealots overthrew the moderate government in Jerusalem. Those suspected of aiding the Romans were arrested or killed, and anti-Roman groups occupied the city. But in March 67 CE, Vespasian marched against the Jewish population. He subjugated Transjordan, western Judea, Idumea, Samaria and Jericho. The only parts of the country remaining in Jewish hands were Jerusalem and seven Herodian fortresses in other parts of the country. After Nero's death in 68 CE, Vespasian's son Titus led the Judean campaign. Just before Passover in April 70, Titus encamped outside the walls of Jerusalem. In late May the Romans occupied the newer part of Jerusalem, north of the temple. By the end of July they took the citadel adjacent to the temple. A week later the porticos surrounding the temple court-yards were burned, and on 28 August the temple went up in flames during the fighting.

After another month the Romans captured the upper city west of the temple, and thus the entire city was taken. All resistance ceased, and Titus ordered Jerusalem be devastated. For the rest of the year, Titus held celebrations in various cities of the near east during which Jewish prisoners were thrown to wild animals or were forced to fight with gladiators. In 71 CE Titus and Vespasian held a triumphal procession in which ritual objects and rebel leaders were exhibited. The Roman conquest of Judea brought about enormous destruction and the enslavement of thousands of Jews.

Despite the devastating victory of the Romans in the first century CE, Jewish revolts continued into the next century. When the emperor Trajan invaded the east up to the Persian coast, uprisings among Babylonian Jews took place. Moreover, riots occurred in many parts of the Roman diaspora. Between 114 and 117 CE Jewish centres in Alexandria, Cyrenaica, Egypt and Cyprus were decimated. In Judea a messianic revolt was led in 132 CE by Simeon Bar Kokhba which appears to have been aided by Akiva and other scholars from Javneh and sparked off by Hadrian's programme of Hellenization. This Jewish revolt was inspired by the conviction that God would empower the Jews to regain control of their country and rebuild the temple. Yet despite the valiant efforts on the part of the rebels, the Romans crushed this uprising. It appears that hundreds of thousands of Jews were killed and Judea was almost completely devastated. In 135 the rebellion came to an end with the fall of Bethar, southwest of Jerusalem. During the course of the campaign Bar Kokhba was killed in battle, and Akiva was later flayed alive.

These two disastrous defeats constituted a profound challenge to the leaders of Jewry. With the loss of their country and the destruction of their sacred place of worship, how were the Jewish people to survive? During this period it appears that the Sadducees and Essenes disappeared. In their place the Pharisees became the dominant religious group, led by Rabban Johanan ben Zakkai, who escaped from Jerusalem during the siege. In the town of Javneh near the Judean sea coast Johanan ben Zakkai assembled a group of distinguished pharisaic scholars (*Tannaim*). There these sages engaged in the development of the legal tradition. Under Johanan ben Zakkai, and later in the century under Rabban Gamaliel II, the rabbinic assembly (*Sanhedrin*) summarized the teachings of the earlier schools of Hillel and Shammai. In addition, they determined the canon of scripture, organized the daily prayers, and transferred to the synagogue some of the observances of the temple, such as the rituals associated with the pilgrim festivals, the Passover *seder*, and the blowing of the ram's horn at the New Year. They also instituted a procedure of rabbinic ordination.

Though this body was presided over by a head (*nasi*), the scholars collectively reached decisions which were binding on the populace. Its members were drawn from all sectors of society and they attracted numerous students to hear their oral teachings. The first generation of sages was followed by a second generation of eminent scholars. The most prominent scholar of the first decades of the second century was Akiva who was an exegete, mystic and legal systematizer as well as a pioneer of a method of scriptural interpretation based on the view that no word in scripture is redundant.

This reorientation of Jewish life brought about a regeneration of Judaism in both Judea and the diaspora.

Without a homeland and a central place of worship, Jews were bound together by the institutions that emerged following the destruction of the temple. By the third century CE economic conditions in Galilee had improved and the Jewish population attained harmonious relations with the Roman administration. The Severan dynasty of Roman emperors entrusted the *nasi* with the authority to appoint judges for Jewish courts, collect taxes and send messengers to diaspora communities. The most important *nasi* of this epoch was Judah Ha-Nasi whose main achievement was the redaction of the *Mishnah*.

This volume consisted of the discussions and rulings of scholars whose teachings had been transmitted orally. The *Mishnah* itself is almost entirely *halakhic* in content, consisting of six sections (or orders) comprising a series of chapters on specific subjects. In addition a tractate of rabbinic moral maxims – Sayings of the Fathers – is included. The *Sanhedrin* which had been so fundamental in the compilation of this work met in several cities in Galilee, but later settled in the Roman district of Tiberias. The *nasi* remained the head of the *Sanhedrin* but other scholars established their own schools in other parts of the country where they applied the *Mishnah* to everyday life together with old rabbinic teachings, *baraitot*, which had not been incorporated into the *Mishnah*.

By the first half of the fourth century, Jewish scholars in *Eretz Israel* had collected together the teachings of generations of rabbis in the academies of Tiberias, Caesarea and Sepphoris. These extended discussions of the *Mishnah* became the Palestinian *Talmud*. The text of this multivolume work covered four sections of the *Mishnah*. The views of these Palestinian teachers (*Amoraim*) had an important influence on scholars in Babylonia, though this work never attained the same prominence as that of the Babylonian *Talmud*.

In the diaspora Babylonian Jewry continued to prosper after the destruction of Jerusalem. From the sixth century BCE when Nebuchadnezzar deported Jews from their native land, Babylonia had become an important centre of Jewish life. By the second century CE, the Persian king who had become overlord of Mesopotamia recognized the exilarch as leader of the Jewish community. This figure collected taxes, appointed judges, supervised the judiciary and represented the Jewish population in the Persian royal court. By the middle of this century rabbinic Judaism spread eastwards and some Palestinian scholars temporarily settled in Babylonia during the Bar Kokhba revolt and Hadrian's persecutions. Subsequently a number of Babylonian Jews went to the centres of learning in Galilee to study under the leading sages in the Holy Land.

The codification of the *Mishnah* further intensified such interchange. In this context the exilarch encouraged the emergence of a Babylonian class of scholars from whom he appointed administrators and judges. While post-*Mishnaic* scholars in Israel engaged in learned debate about the application of Jewish law, the same development was taking place in Babylonia. The third-century teacher Rav founded an academy at Sura in central Mesopotamia; his contemporary Samuel was simultaneously head of another Babylonian academy at Nehardea. After Nehardea was destroyed in 259, the school at

Pumbeditha also became a dominant Babylonian academy of Jewish learning.

The religious leaders of the Babylonian Jewish community were revered for their learning and the academies they founded became major centres of Jewish scholarship. The Babylonian sages carried on and developed the Galilean tradition of disputation and the fourth century produced two of the most distinguished scholars of the *Amoraic* period – Abbaye and Rava who both taught at Pumbeditha. With the decline of Jewish institutions in Israel, Babylonia became the most important centre of Jewish scholarship. By the sixth century Babylonian sages completed the redaction of the *Talmud*, an editorial task begun by Rav Ashi at Sura.

This massive work parallels the Palestinian *Talmud* and is largely a summary of the *Amoraic* discussions that took place in the Babylonian academies. Both *Talmud*s are essentially elaborations of the *Mishnah* though neither commentary contains material on every *Mishnah* passage. In this compilation conflicting opinions of the earlier sages are contrasted, unusual words are explained, and anonymous opinions are identified. Frequently, individual teachers cite specific cases to support their views and hypothetical eventualities are examined to reach a solution to the discussion. Debates between outstanding scholars in one generation are often cited, as are differences of opinion between contemporary members of an academy or a teacher and his students. The scope of *Talmudic* exploration is much broader than that of the *Mishnah* itself and includes a wide range of rabbinic teachings about theology, philosophy and ethics.

This effloresence of Jewish life in *Eretz Israel* and Babylonia was the direct result of the Roman onslaught against Judaism and the Jewish people. Rather than destroy Jewish life, persecution and exile brought about a spiritual revolution. Under the leadership of pharisaic teachers, the Jewish people survived this tragedy. For the second time they were led into exile, yet Jewish existence continued and flourished. New institutions were created, and the study of the law served as a unifying force, binding together the Jewish nation. Scattered communities in the diaspora looked to rabbinic sages for leadership, as Babylonian and Palestinian sages engaged in discussions of the divine commandments. Hence, as in previous centuries, Jew-hatred brought about a revival of Jewish existence and intensified dedication to the Jewish heritage.

14

THE CHURCH AND THE JEWS

As we have seen, Judeophobia was common in Hellenized society. Yet, Jew-hatred, which was prevalent in the Greco-Roman world, intensified within the Christian community. Jesus' messiahship was understood as ushering in a new era in which the true Israel would become a light to the nations. Christian animosity was fuelled by the Gospel writers, who depicted Jesus attacking the leaders of the nation. Further, the Church taught that what was now required was circumcision of the heart rather than obedience to the law. Despite such hostility, Jews remained loyal to their ancient heritage and prospered in the diaspora. In Babylonia and *Eretz Israel* the academies flourished, and in later centuries the study of the *Talmud* reached great heights. In addition, Jewish scholars produced philosophical treatises in which they defended Judaism as the one true faith.

CHRISTIAN ANTI-SEMITISM

In proclaiming the good news, Paul emphasized that the Hebrew people had been rejected by God; Christ is the true eternal temple in opposition to the earthly cult in Jerusalem. Such a contrast is also found in the fourth Gospel which differentiates between the spiritual universe of Christianity and a fallen world represented by the Jews.

Following New Testament teaching, the early Church fathers developed an *Adversos Judaeos* tradition that flourished from the second to the sixth centuries. This malevolent polemic against the Jews is found in treatises, sermons and discourses as well as other types of literature which seek to illustrate that the Jews were rejected by God. Such hostility was based on the claim that the Jews had refused to accept Jesus as Messiah and Saviour. For the Church fathers, this was not an act of apostasy; instead the Jews had *always* been an apostate nation. The patriarchs were righteous individuals; however, with the Egyptian sojourn the ancient Israelites engaged in various types of evil acts. The aim of Mosaic legislation is to curtail such depravity.

In the promised land, the nation continued their idolatrous behaviour. The third-century African Church father Tertullian wrote in his *An Answer to the Jew* that according to scripture the Jewish people forsook God and did degrading service to idols. They abandoned God and prostrated themselves before images. In later times when kings ruled over them, they worshipped calves and enslaved themselves to the Canaanite Baal. In the fourth century the Syrian exegete and ecclesiastical writer Ephrem in *Rhythm Against the Jews* also accused the Jews of idolatry, contending that the persecution of Christ was prefigured in previous times.

In early Christian sources, the Jews were also charged

with blaspheming against God's nature, resisting his spirit, and engaging in sensual excess. Again, in *Eight Orations Against the Jews*, the fourth-century Christian theologian and preacher John Chrysostom linked such behaviour with the rejection of God. In his view, the ancient Hebrews were debauchers and idolators who sacrificed their children to demons and ate their sons and daughters. Such practices justified God's rejection of the Jewish people. In the third century, in his *Expository Treatise Against the Jews*, the Roman ecclesiastical writer Hippolytus summarized their fall from grace. Why was the temple made desolate, he asked. Was it because of their worship of the golden calf? Was it because of their idolatry? Was it because the prophets' blood had been spilled? Was it because of the Jewish people's adultery and fornication? These were not the reason, he stated, because pardon was always open to them. Rather, it was because they killed the son who is co-eternal with the Father.

Moreover, previous crimes which had characterized the ancient Hebrews were viewed to have continued to the present day. Just as Jews were responsible in previous centuries for their sins, so they were equally guilty of iniquity in contemporary circumstances. In his sermons John Chrysostom emphasized that the Jews continued to be a lawless and dissolute people, destined to evoke God's wrath. With venom, he attacked the Jewish community of his own age. Jews, he declared, are no better than pigs or goats, and they live by the rule of debauchery. For Chrysostom and others, the Jews are not human beings; they are demons incarnate who had been cast off by God into utter darkness.

According to early Church fathers, prophetic denunciations in scripture against iniquity apply to the Jewish people; however all future promises relate to adherents of the true Church. Given this interpretation, scripture bears witness to a catalogue of Jewish sins. In his *Tract Against the Jews*, the fourth-century theologian Augustine maintained that the Jewish nation is incapable of understanding the the nature of the Bible: they believe the divine promises apply to the Jewish people. But, Augustine asserted, the Jews are the enemies of God. When the prophets declared that God has cut off the house of Israel, these pronouncements refer to the Jews. When Israel is described positively, these statements apply to the Christian Church.

Viewed, thus, both apostate Jews and the universal Church were anticipated in the Hebrew Bible. Those who are righteous belong to the Christian community. The Jews, however, are the enemies referred to in the psalms and the suffering servant passages in Isaiah. In formulating this view, Christian scholars understood the account of Jacob and Esau as prefiguring these two religious groups. Genesis declares that 'When her [Rebekah's] days to be delivered were fulfilled, behold, there were twins in her womb ... and two peoples, born of you, shall be divided; the one shall be stronger than the other, the elder shall serve the younger (Genesis 25:23–4). Here 'the elder' refers to the Jews who will serve 'the younger' (the Church).

In presenting their views, the Church fathers appealed to Paul's doctrine that the true sons of Abraham are those who are justified by faith. Hence, the descendants of

Abraham are not the Jews, but the Gentiles. As the fifth-century theologian Isaac of Antioch declared in *Homilies Against the Jews*, the uncircumcised Gentiles have taken Israel's place. As in the New Testament, patristic literature interpreted those passages describing Israel as a light to the nations as prophecies about the Church. The Church fathers also maintained that the election of Gentiles is the culmination of the messianic vision of the ingathering of the nations to Zion. According to patristic tradition, the Jewish nation is destined to suffer numerous calamities. Because of their refusal to accept Christ, they are cast out and despised. In his *Demonstrations of the Gospel*, the fourth-century theologian Eusebius declared that because of their impiety, their kingdom was utterly destroyed, the *Torah* abrogated, and ancient worship uprooted. Their royal city, he wrote, was burned with fire, and the holy altar consumed with flames. In this process, the Jewish nation was dispersed among the nations and with no hope of deliverance.

In their writings, the Church fathers utilized the book of Daniel to illustrate that the Jews were to endure captivity. Both the Egyptian and Babylonian captivities were limited in time, but there will be no future liberation from exile due to the Jewish refusal to accept Christ. No Messiah will deliver them from their wandering. The third-century Roman theologian Hippolytus explained in his *Expository Treatise Against the Jews* that the Jews wander as in the night, and stumble on places with no roads. They fall headlong because of their rejection of the Redeemer. They will not be bound to 430 years servitude in Egypt, or 70 years in Babylonia, but their plight will last forever.

The early Christian assault on Judaism and the Jewish community had a profound impact on Jewish life. By the fifth century, the status of Jews had been transformed. In the eyes of the Church, the Jew was regarded as a representative of Satan – an obstinate unbeliever, subject to God's wrath. Christian anti-Judaism had thus been accorded official approval by the Church. Jewish souls could be saved, but only if they embrace Christ. Yet, those who remained obdurate were lost forever. The growth of Christian anti-Semitism from New Testament times was thus rooted in the conflict between these two rival faiths, both seeing themselves as the true Israel. Both religions laid claim to being God's chosen people, the recipients of his revelation. Yet, now that Christianity had become the religion of the empire, Jews were defenceless against this Christian onslaught.

Nonetheless, Judaism flourished in the diaspora. In Babylonia, the academies of Sura and Pumbeditha were centres of Jewish learning as were the academies in Palestine. By the sixth century CE, the Palestinian and Babylonian *Talmuds* had been completed, recording the deliberations of Jewish sages through the ages. Elsewhere in Western Europe Jews lived in small, self-contained enclaves and engaged in local trades. The Jews in each town constituted a separate unit since there was no equivalent of an *exilarch* as in Muslim lands to serve as the official leader of the Jewish population. Each community established its own rules and administered local courts, in the form of self-government which was the Ashkenazic adaptation to the feudal structure of medieval Christian Europe. In this environment Jewish study took place in a number of important centres such as Mainz and Worms in the Rhineland and Troyes and Sens in northern France and produced such leading scholars as the legal expert Rabbenu Gershom of Mainz and the greatest commentator of the medieval period, Solomon ben Isaac of Troyes (Rashi). In subsequent generations, the study of the *Talmud* reached great heights: in Germany and northern France scholars known as the *tosafists* utilized new methods of *talmudic* interpretation. In addition, Ashkenazic Jews of this period composed religious poetry modelled on the liturgical compositions of fifth- and sixth-century Israel.

In addition, Jewish scholars during this period produced a wide range of philosophical studies in which they extolled Judaism as the one true faith. The beginnings of Jewish philosophical speculation took place in ninth-century Babylonia during the height of the Abbasid caliphate when rabbinic Judaism was challenged by Karaite scholars who criticized the anthropomorphic views of God in rabbinic literature. Added to this internal threat was the Islamic contention that Muhammad's revelation in the *Qur'an* superseded the Jewish faith. In addition, Zoroastrians and Manicheans attacked monotheism as a viable religious system. Finally some Gentile philosophers argued that the Greek scientific and philosophical worldview could account for the origin of the cosmos without any reference to an external diety.

To combat these challenges, Saadiah Gaon, as *gaon* of one of the Babylonian academies, attempted to refute the religious claims of Christians, Muslims and Zoroastrians. Later, the Neo-Platonic theologian Solomon ben Joseph ibn Gabirol argued in *The Fountain of Life* that God and matter are not opposed as two ultimate principles. For ibn Gabirol the universe consists of cosmic existences flowing out of the superabundant light and goodness of the creator. Another important Spanish writer of this period, Bahya ben Joseph ibn Pakuda, drew on Neo-Platonic ideas in the composition of his ethical work, *Duties of the Heart.* In this work, he sought to lead Jews through various ascending stages of the inner life towards spiritual perfection. Another important philosopher of this period, Abraham ibn Daud in *The Exalted Faith*, utilized Aristotelian categories in attempting to harmonize the Bible with rational thought.

In opposition to such rationalistic formulations of Jewish belief, the contemporary Spanish theologian Judah Halevi composed a treatise, *The Book of the Khazars*, to demonstrate that Judaism cannot be understood by the intellect alone. This work consists of a dialogue between a king of the Khazars and a Jewish sage who defends the Jewish faith against Aristotelian philosophy, Christianity and Islam. For Halevi biblical revelation rather than philosophy offers the true guide to the spiritual life. The development of Jewish philosophy – coupled with the outpouring of rabbinic literature – illustrates the vibrancy of Judaism despite the oppressive and destructive impact of Christian opposition to the Jewish faith. Although Jews were without a country of their own, they were united as a faith community in the scattered settlements of the diaspora.

JEW-HATRED AND MEDIEVAL CHRISTENDOM

Living among Christians, the Jewish population was despised in the Middle Ages. The practice of usury intensified anti-Semitism especially by those who were unable to pay back loans. Added to this economic motive, Christians in the Middle Ages persecuted Jews on religious grounds: the Jew was stereotyped as a demonic Christ-killer and murderer. Jews were accused of killing Christian children at Passover to use their blood in the preparation of unleavened bread; in addition, they were charged with defaming the host in order to torture Jesus' body. Despite such contempt, medieval Jewish scholarship reached great heights: during this period Jewish philosophers, mystics and rabbinic sages produced works of great distinction.

JEWS IN THE MIDDLE AGES

The tradition of anti-Semitism created by the fathers of the Church continued into the Middle Ages. In the fifth and sixth centuries the Church issued legislation as contained in the *Codex Theodosianus* and the Justinian

Code which denied Jews numerous rights. Repeatedly Church officials warned against the pernicious influence of the Jewish population and at times attempted to convert them by force. In the ninth century Archbishop Agobard of Lyons wrote a number of anti-Jewish epistles in which he expressed alarm about Christian contact with those of the Jewish faith.

Shortly after 1000, rumours began to circulate in Christian lands about the 'Prince of Babylon' who had brought about the destruction of the holy sepulchre in Jerusalem and the persecution of Christians at the instigation of the Jews. In response, princes, bishops and townsfolk sought revenge against Jews, and attacks took place in Rouen, Orleans, Limoges, Mainz and elsewhere. Jews were converted by force or massacred. At the end of the eleventh century, Pope Urban II preached the first crusade at the Council of Clermont-Ferrand. As Christian knights, monks and commoners set out on their holy mission, they took revenge on Jewish infidels living in Christian lands. In 1146 Pope Eugenius III and St Bernard of Clairvaux preached a new crusade which was accompanied by anti-Jewish sentiment.

In the twelfth century Jews were accused of murdering Christian children to incorporate their blood in the preparation of unleavened bread for Passover. The first case of a suspected ritual murder took place in 1144 in Norwich, England. The body of a young apprentice was discovered on the evening of Good Friday in a wood. It was rumoured he had been killed by Jews in imitation of Christ's passion. According to tradition, this murder had been planned by a meeting of rabbis which took place at

Narbonne. Although the Church authorities attempted to protect the Jewish population, riots took place and a leading Jewish figure was killed. Three years later a different allegation appeared – Jews were censured for profaning the Host. As Jean d'Outremeuse, the chronicler of Liege, wrote:

> In this year, it happened at Cologne that the son of a converted Jew went on Easter day to church, in order to receive the body of God, along with the others; he took it into his mouth and quickly bore it to his house; but when he returned from the church, he grew afraid and in his distress made a hole in the earth and buried the Host within it; but a priest came along, opened the hole, and in it found the shape of a child, which he intended to bear to the church; but there came from the sky a great light, the child was raised out of the priest's hands and borne up to heaven.[1]

In 1215, the Fourth Lateran Council promulgated a series of decrees affecting the Jewish community. Nearly 1,500 churchmen from throughout the Christian world endorsed the decisions taken by Pope Innocent. Regarding Jewish clothing, the Council stated:

> In the countries where Christians do not distinguish themselves from Jews ... it is decreed that henceforth Jews of both sexes will be distinguished from other peoples by their garments, as moreover has been prescribed unto them by Moses.[2]

The enforcement of such provisions differed from country to country. In France a circular badge of yellow cloth was worn. In Germany a particular type of hat was worn rather than a badge of clothing. In Poland Jews were required to wear a pointed green hat, whereas in England stripes of cloth were sewn across the chest often in the shape of tablets of the law. In Spain and Italy an insignia was worn. These various marks impressed on the minds of Gentiles the differences between Christians and Jews, encouraging Jews to be regarded as a different species from ordinary humans.

During this period the Church took an interest in Jewish sources, particularly the *Talmud*. An apostate of Judaism, Nicholas Donin, travelled to Rome to inform Pope Gregory IX that the *Talmud* contains blasphemies against the Christian faith. As a consequence the pope urged the kings of France, England, Castile and Aragon to investigate this claim. In France, Louis IX initiated such an investigation, and throughout the country copies of the *Talmud* were confiscated. In 1240 a public debate was held in Paris between leading churchmen and Jewish scholars. As a result, the *Talmud* was condemned and burned.

Throughout the Middle Ages, the Jewish community was detested and the stereotype of the demonic Jew became part of western culture. Repeatedly during this period Jews were accused of possessing attributes of both the devil and witches. In the activities of the Jews the devil's hand was seen at work – the Jew-devil stalked Europe, seeking Christians as his prey. Accused of sorcery, Jewish doctors in particular were seen as agents of the demonic realm. Viewed as evil magicians, they were condemned by the Church. In the light of this conception of the Jew-devil, the Jews were depicted in medieval chronicles as predators who sought to destroy the entire social life of the communities where they lived.

Hated by Gentiles, Jewish communities turned inwards and formed their own closed worlds. Rather than collapse in the face of persecution and murder, Jews throughout Europe flourished under oppression. The early Jewish communities in Western Europe lived in small, self-contained communities and engaged in local trades. The Jews in each town constituted a separate unit; each community (*kahal*) established its own rules and administered local courts, in a form of self-government which was the Ashkenazic adaptation to the feudal structure of medieval Christian Europe. Alongside Jewish scholarship, Jews in the Rhineland also engaged in mystical study. During the twelfth and thirteenth centuries, the Hasidei Ashkenaz delved into mystical texts as well as philosophical works of such scholars as Saadiah Gaon and various Spanish and Italian Jewish Neo-Platonists. Among the greatest figures of this period were the twelfth-century Samuel ben Kalonymus of Speyer, his son Judah ben Samuel of Regensburg and Eleazer ben Judah of Worms who composed the treatise *The Secret of Secrets*. In their writings these mystics were preoccupied with the mystery of divine unity. God himself, they believed, cannot be known by human reason – thus all anthropomorphic depictions of God in scripture should be understood as referring to God's glory which was formed out of divine fire. This divine glory – *kavod* – was revealed to the prophets and is made manifest to mystics in different ways through the ages. The aim of German mysticism was to attain a vision of God's glory through the cultivation of the life of pietism which embraced devotion, saintliness and contemplation. Pietism made the highest demands on the devotee in terms of humility and altruism. The ultimate sacrifice for these Hasidim was martyrdom, and during this period there were ample opportunities for Jews to die in this way in the face of Christian persecution.

Parallel with these developments in Germany, Jewish mystics in southern France engaged in mystical speculation about the nature of God, the soul, the existence of evil, and the religious life. In twelfth-century Provence, the earliest kabbalistic test, the *Bahir*, reinterpreted the concept of the *sefirot* as depicted in the *Sefer Yetsirah*. In Gerona, the traditions of Issac the Blind were broadly disseminated. The most famous figure of this circle was Moses ben Nahman, known as Nahmanides, who helped this mystical school gain general acceptance. His involvement in kabbalistic speculation combined with his *halakhic* authority persuaded many Jews that mystical teachings were compatible with rabbinic Judaism.

During the time that these Geronese mystics were propounding their kabbalistic theories, different mystical schools of thought developed in other parts of Spain. Influenced by the Hasidei Ashkenaz and the Sufi traditions of Islam, Abraham ben Samuel Abulafia wrote meditative texts concerning the technique of combining the letters of the alphabet as a means of realizing human aspirations towards prophecy. Another Spanish kabbalist, Isaac ibn Latif, sought to elaborate ideas found in Maimonides' *Guide for the Perplexed*. Other Spanish kabbalists were attracted to Gnostic ideas. The mingling of Gnostic teaching with the kabbalah of Gerona resulted in the publication of the major mystical work of Spanish Jewry, the *Zohar*, composed by Moses de Leon in Guadalajara. Although the author places the work in a second-century CE setting, focusing on Rabbi Simeon bar Yochai and his disciples, the doctrines of the *Zohar* are of a much later origin.

Alongside such mystical speculation, Jewish scholars also produced philosophical studies during these centuries. In Muslim Spain such figures as Solomon ibn Gabirol, Bahya ibn Pakuda, Abraham ibn Daud, Judah Halevi and Moses Maimonides had made major contributions to Jewish thought. By the thirteenth century most of the important philosophical texts had been translated into Hebrew by Jews living in southern France. The most prominent Jewish philosopher after Maimonides who was attracted to Aristotelianism was Gersonides. Originally from Provence, he wrote works on a wide range of topics including mathematics, astronomy, law and philosophy. In later centuries, other Jewish philosophers continued the tradition of philosophical speculation.

Christian contempt for Jewry thus did not overwhelm the Jewish communities living under Christian domination. Instead, Jewish life flourished despite oppressive conditions. In the face of contempt and hostility, the Jewish nation remained faithful to their ancestral heritage. Even in the most horrendous circumstances, Jews turned to God to deliver them from their enemies. During the crusades, for example, when the local population was threatened by death, they sacrificed themselves rather than embrace the Christian faith. Here *Kiddush ha-Shem* (Martyrdom for the Divine Name) symbolizes triumph even in death:

> Emico, the wicked, the enemy of the Jews, came with his whole army against the city gate, and the citizens opened it up for him. Then the enemies of the Lord said to each other: 'Look! They have opened up the gate for us. Now let us avenge the blood of 'the hanged one.' The children of the holy covenant who were there, martyrs who feared the Most High, although they saw the great multitude, an army numerous as the sand on the shore of the sea, still clung to their Creator ... As soon as the enemy came into the courtyard they found some of the very pious there with our brilliant master, Isaac ben Moses. He stretched out his neck, and his head they cut off first. The others, wrapped in their fringed prayershawls, sat by themselves in the courtyard, eager to do the will of their Creator. They did not care to flee into the chamber to save themselves for this temporal life, but out of love they received upon themselves the sentence of God.[3]

16

THE INQUISITION AND SECRET JEWS

In medieval Spain anti-Jewish sentiment became a serious problem. Initially hatred was directed against those Jews who had been forcibly converted to Christianity but continued to practise Judaism in secret. In 1480 King Ferdinand and Queen Isabella established the Inquisition to determine if such charges were valid. Inquisitors used torture to extract confessions, and thousands of *conversos* were subsequently convicted and burned at the stake. This terrible period of Jewish history testifies to the Jewish determination to remain loyal to the Jewish heritage even in the most oppressive conditions.

MARRANOS

By the end of the fourteenth century Jews in Spain had come to be regarded with suspicion and contempt. A large number (known as *conversos* or Marranos) embraced the Christian faith in order to escape attack. In the next century the Church embarked on a new form of persecution. The Inquisition was established under Ferdinand and Isabella to purge *conversos* who were suspected of living secretly as Jews. In 1478 a papal bull was promulgated that created the Castilian Inquisition; several years later the first tribunal was established in Seville. Once the Inquisition was formally instituted, the tribunal requested that heretics confess to their crimes. This 'Edict of Grace' lasted for 30 days – those who came forward were obliged to denounce all other Judaizers. In compensation, they were spared torture and imprisonment. They atoned by flagellation, wearing the *sambenito* (sackcloth), and confiscation of their possessions. In addition, they were barred from holding office, practising a profession, or wearing formal dress.

The next stage of the inquisitorial process involved the naming of suspects. An edict was issued which outlined various ways that such individuals could be recognized. Judaizers, it explained, celebrated Jewish festivals, kept the dietary laws, consumed meat during Lent, omitted the phrase 'Glory be to the Father, and to the Son, and to the Holy Ghost' at the end of psalms, and cooked with oil. Once suspects were identified, the Inquisitors attempted to extract a confession. To achieve this end, various tortures were used, interspersed with kind words such as, 'I pity you when I see you so abused and with a lost soul ... So do not assume the sin of others ... admit the truth to me, for, as you see, I already know everything ... In order that I may be able to pardon you and free you soon, tell me who led you to this error.'

During the Inquisition, torture was frequently used to extract confessions. When this was achieved, the Inquisitors were satisfied. However, the innocent suffered more than those who remained loyal to Judaism in secret. Typical of the procedures used by the Inquisitors was the case of Elvira del Campo who was accused by the authorities of Judaizing. As the report concerning her trial explains: 'She was carried to the torture chamber and told to tell the truth when she said that she had nothing to say. She was ordered to be stripped and again admonished, but was silent.' Eventually she was stripped and declared her innocence. Yet, fearing what would occur next, she pleaded with the Inquisitors: 'Senores,' she declared, 'I have done all that is said of me and I bear false witness against myself, for I do not want to see myself in such trouble; Please God, I have done nothing.'

Undeterred, the Inquisitors told her not to bring false testimony against herself, but to tell the truth. Her arms were then tied. She said, 'I have told the truth – what have I to tell?' She was again told to tell the truth and stated: 'I have told the truth and have nothing more to tell.' One cord was applied to her arms and twisted. She was then admonished to tell the truth, but again said she had nothing to tell. She then screamed and said, 'I have done all they say.'

The torture then increased in intensity, and more turns of the cord were applied. She cried, 'Loosen me a little that I may remember what I have to tell. I don't know what I have done; I did not eat pork for it makes me sick; I have done everything; loosen me and I will tell the truth.' Another turn of the cord was ordered, and she was told to explain in detail what she had done. She said, 'What am I expected to tell? I did everything – loosen me for I don't remember what I have to tell.' In agony, she cried out, 'Don't you see what a weak woman I am? Oh! Oh! my arms are breaking.'

In Spain and later in Portugal, the judicial sentence of the Inquisitors following such torture was passed in public in the presence of dignitaries and crowds. At these ceremonies, known as *autos da fé*, sermons were preached; the earliest took place in 1481, and they continued until they numbered hundreds of thousands. Over 30,000 suffered the death penalty. However, the burning of heretics did not occur during the *auto da fé* – those found guilty were handed over to the secular authorities who were responsible for their execution at the place of burning.

What was the attitude of the *conversos* themselves? It was not uncommon for *conversos* who practised Judaism in secret to be haunted by a sense of self-reproach since they could not live in accordance with Jewish law. Overcome by remorse, their prayers expressed a strong sense of guilt:

> Lord, I have failed Thee by my meanness and my unworthiness, ruled by my evilness and by my treason in spite of myself. Thou, who has visited me in true justice and hast cherished me like a son, see how I have fallen in a tribulation so great and so perilous, from which I cannot arise or escape. Knowing my guilt, I turn to Thee, Lord, repentant, sighing and weeping, as a son turns to his father, begging Thy holy mercy for forgiveness, that Thou mayest raise me from the great torment and the great tribulation into which I have fallen.[1]

In order to escape from their allegiance to Christianity, a number of *conversos* sought to de-Christianize themselves by following bizarre practices, including fastening a crucifix to their buttocks, or destroying statues of Jesus.

Seeking to escape the Spanish Inquisition, some Jews sought refuge in Portugal. Unlike their Spanish counterparts, these *conversos* imitated the Christian way of life, complying with Catholic rites and attending mass and confession. Nevertheless, they selectively observed various Jewish rituals such as *Yom Kippur* and *Purim*. In addition, they were comforted by various texts, such as the Prayer of Esther which became an important prayer for the Marrano communities: 'I whom you keep among the infidels, you know how much I hate their criminal feasts … this pomp to which I am condemned, this diadem in which I must appear. Alone and in secret I trample them under my feet.'

Large numbers of these secret Jews, passionately devoted to the Jewish faith, fled from oppression. In their quest to find a safe place where they would be able to live openly as Jews, they travelled to a wide variety of lands. The most natural places of refuge were Muslim lands since Muslims were the arch-enemies of the Christians, and the staunchly Catholic Spain and Portugal were particularly detested. Next to Muslim countries, Protestant lands offered an important refuge for fleeing Marranos. As in Ottoman territory, here Catholics were detested, and the Inquisition was seen as a heinous and fearful institution since it was no more tolerant of Protestant heretics than of Marranos. In England, Hamburg, and other German cities, Marranos lived as secret Jews before the Reformation, continuing that way of life long after these areas had broken with Rome since Protestant authorities were not willing to permit Jews to live in their midst. In Hamburg, for example, the settlement of Jews was not authorized until 1612. In England, Marranos settled in London and Bristol but were never officially recognized as Jews. Initially figures such as Manasseh ben Israel sought to secure formal recognition of the Jewish community, but their efforts were unsuccessful. However, when the Crown granted Jews an official charter of protection, such permission further facilitated the development of the Marrano community.

While Marranos settled in Amsterdam at the end of the sixteenth century, they had to wait until 1615 before Jewish settlement was officially allowed. Yet, the Marranos in Amsterdam differed from those in other Protestant countries since they openly practised Judaism from the time of their arrival. Such an open environment encouraged mass emigration and Amsterdam became one of the most important Jewish centres in Europe. In addition, it also served as a refuge for oppressed Jews from other countries including France in 1615 and Eastern Europe after the Polish pogroms of 1648.

Not surprisingly, Catholic lands outside the control of Spain and Portugal did not offer as secure a haven as Ottoman or Protestant countries. Yet, because they were not under the control of the Inquisition of Spain and Portugal, they did provide a place of refuge; nonetheless, local authorities were not free from outside pressure and, as a result, Marranos were not free of danger. In Rome and Ancona, Marrano communities in the sixteenth century prospered under Clement VII, Paul III and Julius III. Under Paul IV they were even guaranteed that if accused of apostasy they would be subject only to papal authority, yet during this period they became subject to the Counter-Reformation and all protection was withdrawn. As a consequence, over 20 Judaizers were burned alive in 1556, 26 others were condemned to the galleys, and 30 others were freed only after paying a fine.

In Florence, it appears that there were some Marranos among the Spanish and Portuguese merchants who traded with Spain and the colonies. In Ferrara, the Marranos formed an important community by the sixteenth century, and they were protected by the dukes until 1581 when Duke Alfonso II allowed many of them to be arrested. Three were sent to Rome to be burned at the stake. In Venice in the fifteenth and sixteenth centuries Marranos were permitted to settle, but were subject to decrees of expulsion. Later, however, Marranos were welcomed, and some theologians claimed that Judaizers were outside the jurisdiction of the Inquisition since they had been baptized by force.

In France Marranos practised Catholicism for two centuries while secretly following Jewish customs. Even though they were referred to as 'New Christians', their loyalty to the Jewish faith was widely accepted. Living in their own quarters, they developed a system of schools as well as communal institutions. As time passed their link to Catholicism became increasingly tenuous, and in 1730 they were officially recognized as Jews. Marranos had also settled in the Aragonese territories of Sicily, Sardinia and Naples as well as in Habsburg territories, colonial territories in the Far East and the Americas. Frequently their position was insecure, particularly where the Inquisition wielded authority.

In these farflung communities, Marranos were often able to play important roles in economic and social life. Such opportunities were important incentives for Marranos to continue living as secret Jews in Catholic lands, rather than practise Judaism publicly. In many cases these individuals were allowed to settle in foreign lands precisely because they played a major role in the economic life of the host country. Some Marranos rose to prominence in international trade, banking and finance. In addition, they were actively engaged in large trading companies such as the Dutch East Indies and West Indies Companies. Further, a number of Marranos made contributions to manufacturing, handicrafts, armaments and shipbuilding. Others dealt in commodities including coral, sugar, tobacco and precious stones. Yet other Marranos were engaged in printing – by the end of the sixteenth century Venice had the leading press, and in the next century Amsterdam became the centre for publishing. Other cities, including Leghorn, Hamburg and London, had important presses, and printing in smaller places added to the dissemination of Jewish culture. Marrano writers, too, made a significant contribution to Jewish life. Hence, despite the torments of the Inquisition, Marranos continued to remain faithful to their Jewish heritage in secret even in the face of torture and burning at the stake.

17

MASSACRE AND THE MYSTICAL MESSIAH

In the early modern period Poland was a centre of scholarship. In the rabbinical academies the method of *hilluk* (the differentiation and reconciliation of rabbinic opinions) generated considerable activity in the study of *talmudic* law. Moreover, a number of scholars collected together the legal interpretations of previous *halakhists*, and commentaries were written on the *Shulkhan Arukh*. Nonetheless, the Polish Jewish community was subject to a series of massacres in the seventeenth century carried out by Cossacks of the Ukraine as well as Crimean Tartars and Ukrainian peasants who rebelled against the Polish nobility. In the face of this devastating assault, the Jewish community believed that messianic deliverance was at hand – this murderous attack gave rise to religious longing and hope for the ultimate redemption of the Jewish nation. When this failed to materialize, the messianic hope was transformed into the aspiration to create a place of refuge for the Jewish people.

THE MYSTICAL MESSIAH

In 1648 Bogdan Chmielnicki was elected *hetman* of the Cossacks and instigated an insurrection against the Polish gentry which had previously oppressed the Cossack population. As administrators of noblemen's estates, Jews were slaughtered in these revolts. Estates and manor houses were destroyed and victims were flayed, burned alive and mutilated. Infants were murdered and cast into wells; women were cut open and sewn up again with live cats thrust into their wounds. According to a contemporary account

> These persons died cruel and bitter deaths. Some were skinned alive and their flesh was thrown to the dogs; some had their hands and limbs chopped off, and their bodies thrown on the highways only to be trampled by wagons and crushed by horses; some had wounds inflicted on them ... some children were pierced by spears, roasted on the fire, and then brought to their mothers to be eaten.[1]

In this massacre thousands of Jews died in towns east of the River Dnieper and elsewhere.

As the Cossacks advanced, the Polish king died and was succeeded by John Casimir who attempted to negotiate with the Cossacks who demanded an independent Ukrainian state. After several more years of battle, Chmielnicki appealed to the Russian allies who invaded northwestern Poland, but by the following year a Polish partisan movement drove back these foreign invaders. Finally in 1667 Russia and Poland signed the Treaty of Adrusovo which distributed the Western Ukraine to Poland, and the Eastern Ukraine and the Smolensk region to Russia. During these years of war the Jewish population was decimated by the various opposing forces: the Cossacks and Ukrainian peasants regarded Jews as representatives of the Polish aristocracy; the Russians who did not allow Jews to settle in the lands joined the Cossack hordes in this slaughter; and the Polish partisans saw Jews as allied with the Swedes.

During this period of persecution, Jewish hopes for deliverance were raised by the emergence of a self-proclaimed messianic king, Shabbatai Zevi. Jews throughout the Jewish world believed that they were living in the final days of redemption, and that their sufferings were the birth pangs of the Messiah. Born in Smyrna into a wealthy family, Shabbatai had received a traditional Jewish education and later engaged in study of the *Zohar*. After leaving Smyrna in the 1650s he spent ten years in various cities in Greece as well as in Istanbul and Jerusalem. Eventually he became part of a kabbalistic group in Cairo and travelled to Gaza where he encountered Nathan Benjamin Levi who believed Shabbatai was the Messiah. In 1665 his Messiahship was proclaimed, and Nathan sent letters to Jews in the diaspora asking them to repent and recognize Shabbatai Zevi as their redeemer. Shabbatai, he announced, would take the Sultan's crown, bring back the lost tribes, and inaugurate the period of messianic redemption.

After a brief sojourn in Jerusalem, Shabbatai went to Smyrna where he encountered strong opposition on the part of some local rabbis. In response he denounced the disbelievers and declared that he was the Anointed of the God of Jacob. This action evoked a hysterical response – a number of Jews fell into trances and had visions of him on a royal throne crowned as King of Israel. In 1666 he journeyed to Istanbul, but on the order of the grand vizier he was arrested and put into prison. Within a short time the prison quarters became a messianic court; pilgrims from all over the world made their way to Istanbul to join in messianic rituals and in ascetic activities. In addition, hymns were written in his honour and new festivals were introduced. According to Nathan, who remained in Gaza, the alteration in Shabbatai's moods from illumination to withdrawal symbolized his soul's struggle with demonic powers; at times he was imprisoned by the powers of evil but at other moments he prevailed against them.

This same year Shabbatai spent three days with the Polish kabbalist, Nehemiah ha-Kohen, who later denounced him to the Turkish authorities. Shabbatai was brought to court and given the choice between conversion and death. In the face of this alternative, he converted to Islam and took on the name Mehemet Effendi. Such an act of apostasy scandalized most of his followers, but he defended himself by asserting that he had become a Muslim in obeisance to God's commands. Many of his followers accepted this explanation and refused to give up their belief. Some thought it was not Shabbatai who had become a Muslim, but rather a phantom who had taken on his appearance; the Messiah himself had ascended to heaven. Others cited biblical and rabbinic sources to justify Shabbatai's action. Nathan explained that the messianic task involved taking on the humiliation of being portrayed as a traitor to his people.

After Shabbatai's act of apostasy, Nathan visited him in the Balkans and then travelled to Rome where he performed secret rites to bring about the end of the papacy. Shabbatai remained in Adrianople and Istanbul where he lived as both Muslim and Jew. In 1672 he was deported to Albania where he disclosed his own kabbalistic teaching to his supporters. After he died in 1676, Nathan declared that Shabbatai had ascended to the supernal world. Eventually, a number of groups continued in their belief that Shabbatai was the Messiah, including a sect, the Doenmeh, who professed Islam but nevertheless adhered to their own traditions. Marrying among themselves, they eventually evolved into antinomian subgroups which violated Jewish sexual laws and asserted the divinity of Shabbatai and their leader, Baruchiah Russo. In Italy several Shabbatean groups also emerged and propagated their views.

The Cossack rebellion against the Jewish population and the emergence of the mystical Messiah is a further illustration of the pattern of hope born of despair. Rather than view the devastation of Polish Jewry as a tragic example of Jew-hatred, it was perceived as the prelude to deliverance. As Sir Paul Rycaut in *History of the Turkish Empire* explained:

> Millions of people were possessed when Shabbatai Zevi first appeared at Smyran and published himself to the Jews for their Messiah, relating the greatness of their approaching kingdom, the strong hand whereby

the God was about to deliver them from bondage, and gather them from all parts of the world. It was strange to see how this fancy took and how fast the report of Shabbatai and his doctrine flew through all parts where Jews inhabited and so deeply possessed them with a belief of their new kingdom and riches, and many of them with promotion to offices of government, renown and greatness; that in all places from Constantinople to Budu, I perceived a strange transport in the Jews, none of them attending to any business, unless to wind up former negotiations and to prepare themselves and their families for a journey to Jerusalem. All their discourses, their dreams and disposal of their affairs tended to no other design but a re-establishment in the Land of Promise, to greatness and glory, wisdom and doctrine of the Messiah.[2]

Not surprisingly Shabbatai's conversion and the failure of the Messiah to appear in subsequent years led to widespread disillusionment with the Jewish messianic hope. As a consequence, the Jewish preoccupation with messianic calculation diminished, and the longing for the Messiah who will lead the Jewish people to the Holy Land and bring about the end of history appeared to many Jews as a misguided aspiration. The belief in the kingdom of God inaugurated by the Messiah-King receded in importance. Yet, this did not diminish the Jewish hope for the creation of a better world. In the place of the coming of the Messiah, the clarion call for liberty, equality and fraternity signified the dawning of a golden age for the Jewish nation.

Within Reform Judaism in particular, the doctrine of messianic redemption was modified in the light of these developments. In the nineteenth century Reform Jews tended to interpret the new liberation in the western world as the first step towards the realization of the messianic dream. For these reformers messianic redemption was understood in this-worldly terms. No longer, according to this view, is it necessary for Jews to pray for a restoration in *Eretz Israel*; rather Jews should view their own countries as Zion and their political leaders as bringing about the messianic age. Such a conviction was enshrined in the Pittsburgh Platform. As we have noted, as a central principle of the Platform, the belief in a personal Messiah was replaced by the concept of a messianic age which would come about through social causes.

These sentiments were shared by secular Zionists who similarly rejected the traditional belief in the coming of the Messiah and the ingathering of the exiles. The early Zionists were determined to create a Jewish homeland even though the Messiah had not yet arrived. Rejecting the religious categories of the past, such figures as Moses Hess, Leon Pinsker and Theodor Herzl pressed for a political solution to the problem of anti-Semitism. In their view, there is no point in waiting for a supernatural intervention to remedy Jewish existence; rather Jews must create their own salvation. As Pinsker explained:

> Nowadays, when in a small part of the earth our brethren have caught their breath and can feel more deeply for the sufferings of their brothers; nowadays, when a number of other dependent and

oppressed nationalities have been allowed to regain their independence, we, too, must not sit even one moment longer with folded hands; we must not admit that we are doomed to play on in the future the hopeless role of the 'wandering Jew' ... it is our bounden duty to devote all our remaining moral force to re-establishing ourselves as a living nation, so that we may finally assume a more fitting and dignified role.[3]

As in previous centuries, Jewish suffering served as the prelude to renewal. The Cossack onslaught against Polish Jewry was seen as part of God's providential plan to rescue his people from destruction. The arrival of Shabbatai Zevi revived Jewish hopes for the triumph of Jewry against their enemies. And in the face of his conversion to Islam, many Jews set aside the supernatural features of Jewish eschatology and hoped instead for the improvement of society through human endeavour. In this quest, they drew on Jewish ideals grounded in scripture and in rabbinic sources. In addition, many Jews looked to the creation of a Jewish homeland as a bulwark against oppression. In their view, the creation of a Jewish state would offer Jews a refuge from the Jew-hatred of the past.

18

Modern Hatred and Zionism

According to secular Zionists, the emancipation of Jewry had been an illusion: Jews were everywhere objects of contempt and hatred. The only solution to the Jewish problem, they argued, was the re-creation of a Jewish homeland in Palestine. By the beginning of the twentieth century a sizeable number of Jews had migrated to Palestine, and in the ensuing years the Jewish community grew considerably. Despite opposition from the indigenous Arab population, the Zionists pressed for the creation of a Jewish commonwealth. Paradoxically, the establishment of the State of Israel was the direct result of centuries of Jew-hatred.

The Jewish State

In the nineteenth century Zionists were preoccupied with the problem of anti-Semitism. Modern secular Zionism begins with the writings of Moses Hess. In 1862 he published *Rome and Jerusalem*, a systematic defence of Jewish nationalism. In this work, he argued that anti-Jewish sentiment is unavoidable. According to Hess, Jews will always remain strangers among the nations – nothing can alter this state of affairs. The only solution to the problem of Jew-hatred is for the Jewish people to come to terms with their national identity. According to Hess, the restoration of Jewish nationalism will not deprive the world of the benefits promoted by Jewish reformers who wish to dissociate themselves from the particularistic dimensions of the Jewish faith. On the contrary, the values of universalism will be championed by various aspects of Judaism's national character. What is required today, Hess asserted, is for Jewry to regenerate the Jewish nation and to keep alive the hope for the political rebirth of the Jewish people.

For Hess, a Jewish renaissance is possible once national life reasserts itself in the Holy Land. In the past the creative energies of the people deserted Israel when Jews became ashamed of their nationality. The holy spirit, he argued, will again animate Jewry once the nation awaken to a new life. The only question remaining is how it might be possible to stimulate the patriotic sentiments of modern Jewry as well as to liberate the Jewish masses by means of this revived national loyalty. This is a formidable challenge, yet Hess maintained that it must be tackled. Although he recognized that there could not be a total emigration of world Jewry to Palestine, Hess believed that the existence of a Jewish state would act as a spiritual centre for the Jewish people and for all of humanity.

The Russian pogroms had a profound impact on another early Zionist, Leon Pinsker, driving him from an espousal of the ideas of the Enlightenment to the determination to create a Jewish homeland. In 1882 he published *Autoemancipation*, in which he argued that the Jewish problem is as unresolved in the modern world as it was in former times. In essence, this dilemma concerns the unassimilable character of Jewish identity in countries where Jews are in the minority. In such cases there is no basis for mutual respect between Jews and non-Jews. Among the nations of the world, Pinsker argued, the Jews are like a nation long since dead. The fear of the Jewish ghost has been a typical reaction throughout the centuries, and has paved the way for current Judeophobia. This prejudice has through the years become rooted and naturalized among all peoples of the world.

Such Jew-hatred has generated various charges against the Jewish people: throughout history Jews have been accused of crucifying Jesus, drinking the blood of Christians, poisoning wells, exacting usury and exploiting peasants. Such accusations are invariably groundless – they were trumped up to quiet the conscience of Jew-baiters. Thus Judaism and anti-Semitism have been inseparable companions through the centuries, and any struggle against this aberration of the human mind is fruitless. Unlike other peoples, the Jews are inevitably aliens. They are not simply guests in a foreign country; they are more like beggars and refugees.

For Pinsker the present moment is a decisive time for the revival of national aspirations. History appears to be on the side of world Jewry in its longing for a national homeland. Even in the absence of a leader like Moses, the recognition of what Jewish people need most should arouse a number of energetic individuals to take on positions of responsibility. Already, he noted, there are societies that are pressing for the creation of a Jewish nation. They must now invoke a national congress and establish a directorate to bring to fruition these plans. Not all Jews will be able to settle in a Jewish homeland. Yet, it will serve as a refuge for those who seek to flee from oppression and persecution.

More than with any other figure, modern secular Zionism has become identified with Theodor Herzl. In *The Jewish State* he argued that his advocacy of a Jewish homeland is not simply a utopian scheme; on the contrary, his plan is a realistic proposal arising out of the appalling conditions facing Jews living under oppression and persecution. The plan, he stated, would be impractical if only a single individual were to undertake it. But if many Jews were to agree on its importance, its implementation would be entirely reasonable. Like Pinsker, Herzl believed that the Jewish question can be solved only if Jews constitute themselves as one people.

Old prejudices against Jewry are ingrained in western society – assimilation will not act as a cure for the ills that beset the Jewish people. There is only one remedy for the malady of anti-Semitism: the creation of a Jewish commonwealth. In *The Jewish State*, Herzl outlined the nature of such a social and political entity. The plan, he stated, should be carried out by two agencies: the Society of Jews and the Jewish Company. The scientific programme and political policies that the Society of Jews will establish should be carried out by the Jewish Company. This body will be the liquidating agent for the business interests of departing Jews, and will organize trade and commerce in the new country. Given such a framework, immigration of Jews will be gradual. Their tasks will be to construct roads, bridges, railways and telephone installations; in addition, they will regulate rivers and provide themselves with homesteads.

This vision grew out of despair at the tragedy of Jewish existence. For these three writers, there is no solution to the predicament of Jewry in modern times. For over 3,000 years, Jews have suffered at the hands of their neighbours. No longer should this intolerable situation occur. What is now required is the establishment of a Jewish common-wealth where Jews will be in the majority. Only in this way will Jewry achieve full emancipation and liberty. Anxious to pursue this vision, Herzl began a campaign to arouse interest in the creation of a Jewish homeland. On 29 August 1897 the First Zionist Congress opened in Basle; over 200 delegates attended, representing 24 states and territories.

In its programme the Congress adopted by accla-mation the quest to establish a Jewish homeland in Palestine. In 1898 a Second Zionism Congress was held at Basle with nearly double the number of participants. In October and November 1898 the Kaiser met Herzl in Constaninople; in his view such a meeting could provide an opportunity to enlist support for the movement, since Imperial Germany was emerging as the patron and protector of the Ottoman empire. During his discussion, Herzl encouraged the Kaiser to ask the sultan if a chartered company for Jews in Palestine under German protection could be created. Initially it appears that the Kaiser viewed this plan favourably, but when he met with a Zionist delegation headed by Herzl in Jerusalem nothing was said about this plan.

At the Third Zionist Congress Herzl stressed that progress had been made towards creating a Jewish state. He had met the Kaiser, and all efforts must now be directed towards obtaining a charter from the Turkish government under the sovereignty of the sultan. Such an agreement would enable Zionists to undertake widespread settlement in Palestine. In pursuit of this aim, Herzl met with the Sultan on 17 May 1901. Despite Herzl's enthusiasm for this meeting, the interview produced no positive results. Undeterred, Herzl concentrated on influencing British opinion. The Fourth Zionist Congress was to be held in London, and Herzl turned his attention to affecting British policy. Giving evidence before the Royal Commission on immigration, he stated that European Jews were subject to increasing anti-Semitism. How were they to escape such persecution? he asked. Emigration would be possible if a Jewish homeland were made available.

Determined to carry on with negotiations, Herzl met with the king of Italy and Pope Pius X in Rome in January 1904 and explained the importance of creating a Jewish settlement in Palestine. The Pope, however, was insistent that the Jewish people embrace the Christian faith if he were to support the notion of a return to the Holy Land. After Herzl's death on 3 July 1904, the Zionist movement continued to press for a Jewish return to *Eretz Israel*. After more than a year of negotiations between the Zionists and the British government, the Balfour Declaration was issued. Such a solution to the Jewish problem was in line with the British aspiration of defeating Turkey and becoming the major power in the Middle East. In a letter from the British Foreign Secretary, Arthur Balfour, to Lord Rothschild, dated 2 November 1917, the British government resolved to create a 'National Home' for the Jewish people in Palestine.

In order to ensure that a Jewish National Home be established, a Jewish delegation headed by Chaim Weizmann addressed the Paris Peace Conference on 27 February 1919. After listening to impassioned speeches by the delegates, the Paris Peace Conference agreed to grant the Palestine Mandate to Great Britain, and accepted the need to establish a Jewish homeland in Palestine as outlined by the Balfour Declaration. In the years following the First World War, a further wave of immigration took place in Palestine; approximately 35,000 Jewish settlers entered the country. These newcomers worked on road-building, set up *kibbutzim* and *moshavim* (villages of smallholders). In order to unify the various Labour Zionist groups that had developed since the First World War, the General Federation of Jewish Labour was founded under the leadership of David Ben Gurion.

These steps towards the creation of a Jewish homeland were met by increasing hostility on the part of the Arab population, which erupted into the 1920 riots. In response, the Jewish community in Palestine agreed that a defence organization was now needed. In March 1921 the *Haganah* was established as a secret body, acting without the consent of the British authorities. Initially it trained members and purchased arms in the quest to defend Jewish property and life. During this period of instability an English Jew, Sir Herbert Samuel, arrived in June 1920 in Palestine as High Commissioner and

Commander in Chief. Although an ardent Zionist, he believed that Jews would be able to live harmoniously with the Arab population.

The emergence of the Zionist movement is a further example of Jewish renewal under pressure. Faced with increasing hostility towards European Jewry, the Jewish people looked to themselves for a solution to the problem of anti-Semitism. As Herzl explained in *The Jewish State*, there is no possibility for Jews to be accepted in the societies where they reside:

> We have sincerely tried everywhere to merge with the national communities in which we live, seeking only to preserve the faith of our fathers. It is not permitted us. In vain we are loyal patriots, sometimes superloyal; in vain do we make the same sacrifices of life and property as our fellow citizens; in vain do we strive to enhance the fame of our native lands in the arts and sciences, or her wealth by trade and commerce. In our native lands where we have lived for centuries we are still decried as aliens ... The majority decide who the 'alien' is; this, and all else in the relations between peoples, is a matter of power.[1]

Old prejudices against Jewry are ingrained in western society. Hence, there is only one remedy for the sickness of anti-Semitism: the creation of a Jewish commonwealth. In the conclusion of this work, Herzl passionately expressed the longing of the entire nation for the establishment of a refuge from centuries of persecution:

What glory awaits the selfless fighters for the cause! Therefore I believe that a wondrous breed of Jews will spring up from the earth. The Maccabees will rise again. Let me repeat once more my opening words: The Jews who will it shall achieve their state. We shall live at last as free men on our own soil, and in our own homes peacefully die. The world will be liberated by our freedom, enriched by our wealth, magnified by our greatness.[2]

The creation of a Jewish homeland was thus born out of Jew-hatred; without anti-Semitism, the State of Israel would not exist – this is the paradox of Jewish history.

19

JEWS, ARABS AND THE JEWISH STATE

Despite the opposition of Palestinian Arabs, Zionism had become an organized movement and Zionists continued to press for the creation of a Jewish homeland. Eventually the British government approved of such a plan although Britain insisted that the rights of the Arabs be safeguarded. Although the British government initially allowed free immigration to Palestine, this policy was superseded by increased restrictions on the number of Jewish immigrants. Such a policy evoked widespread Jewish resistance. After a campaign of terror, Britain handed over the Palestinian problem to the United Nations, and on 14 May 1948 Prime Minister David Ben Gurion read out the Scroll of Independence which declared the right of Israel to exist. After an exile of 2,000 years in which the Jewish community had been persecuted and oppressed, Jews were at long last free in their own country.

THE CREATION OF ISRAEL

During the decades before the First World War, the foundation of Zionist settlements in Palestine evoked considerable Arab hostility. In 1891 a number of prominent Arabs sent a petition to the Ottoman capital in Constantinople requesting the prohibition of Jewish immigration as well as the purchase of land in Palestine. From 1908 to 1914 anti-Zionist newspapers were published in Haifa, Jaffa, Beirut and Damascus. During this period Zionism was viewed in the Arab world as a threat to the 1,300-year-old tradition of Palestine as a Muslim land.

Before the war, Palestinian Arabs were aggravated by Jewish settlers whose socialist ideals clashed with their Islamic traditions. In the 1920s and 1930s Arab leaders complained to the British Mandatory Government that Jewish immigrants were advocating communist principles which led to violence and social change. These radicals, they urged, should be expelled from the country. According to Palestinian critics, Zionism was equated with communism, and the Jewish character was seen as inherently subversive. Such attitudes were influenced by various anti-Semitic tracts such as the forged *Protocols of the Elders of Zion* which stressed that communism is part of the Jewish plot for obtaining world domination.

Palestinian arguments against Zionism concentrated on the need to ensure the self-determination of the Muslim community. In their defence, Palestinians appealed to the principle of the right of all peoples to protect their national identity. At the time of the Balfour Declaration, they pointed out, 90 per cent of the population in Palestine were Arabs; Palestine was a Holy Land to millions of Arabs worldwide; the Arabs had lived there since the seventeenth century. Initially the Arab nationalist movement distinguished between the indigenous Jewish populace whom they esteemed, and foreign Zionists who were seen as interlopers. However, this distinction was not long lasting, and in the Arab demonstrations of February and March 1920 all Jews were condemned.

In April 1920 Arab mobs in Jerusalem attacked Jewry in the Jewish quarter of the Old City. This massacre was a result of the inflammatory address by the Grand Mufti in Jerusalem, Haj Amin al-Husseini. From 1920 Haj Amin attempted to provoke Jew-hatred by claiming that the Jews wished to occupy the Temple Mount area in order to rebuild Solomon's temple. In 1929 such agitation resulted in pogroms in Hebron and Safed in which about 100 Orthodox Jews were killed. This uprising was presented as an anti-imperialist revolt and a victory for the Arab world. In the 1930s a popular national movement was founded which brought the Palestinan cause to the forefront of Pan-Arab concerns. During this period the rise of Nazi Germany intensified Judeophobia in Arab lands. Hitler was admired in the Arab world as a nationalist leader who had humiliated Britain and France. After Hitler acceded to power, Haj Amin joined forces with the Nazis and planned a boycott against the Jews.

Arab hostility to the quest to establish a Jewish state in Palestine did not subdue Jewish aspirations. Instead, the earlier settlers were determined to overcome Arab opposition as well as the harsh conditions of the country. Following the pogroms in Russia at the end of the nineteenth century, members of *Hovevei Zion* emigrated to Palestine where they established farms and villages. During the First *Aliyah* from 1882 to 1903 about 25,000 Jews reached Palestine. In 1906 the first Hebrew high school was founded in Jaffa. Two years later, Arthur Ruppin became head of the Palestine Office of the Zionist Executive and encouraged the creation of Jewish farming settlements. During this period Tel Aviv was founded north of Jaffa. In 1911 the first Jewish hospital was opened in Haifa. In subsequent years *kibbutizim* and *moshavim* were established throughout the country.

In the face of growing opposition, the Jewish community in Palestine defended itself from attack. In 1929 a massacre took place in Palestine in which 150 Jews were killed; this led to a further limit on immigration despite the fact that hundreds of thousands of Jews sought entry into Palestine. As more and more Jews were allowed to settle, Arab resentment intensified. Each year there were more than 30,000 arrivals, and in 1935 the number grew to 62,000. In response, in April 1936 a major Arab uprising took place. On 7 July 1937 a commission headed by Lord Peel recommended that Jewish immigration be reduced to 12,000 a year, and restrictions were placed on land purchases. In addition, a three-way partition was suggested. This plan was rejected by the Arabs, and another revolt took place in 1937. In the following year, the Pan-Arab conference in Cairo adopted a policy whereby all Arab communities pledged that they would take action to prevent further Zionist expansion.

After the failure of the tripartite plan in London

in 1939 the British abandoned the policy of partition. In May 1939 a new White Paper was published stating that only 75,000 more Jews could be admitted over five years, and thereafter none except with Arab agreement. At the same time Palestine should proceed with plans to become independent. Although the Jews supported the allies, Jewry was committed to overturning British policy as enshrined in the 1939 White Paper. During this period the British attempted to prevent illegal immigrants from landing in Palestine; if their ships got through they were captured and deported.

In 1943 Menahem Begin took over control of the Revisionist military army, the *Irgun*. With 600 agents under his control, he blew up various British buildings. On 6 November 1944 the ultra-extreme group, the Stern Gang, murdered Lord Moyne, the British Minister for Middle Eastern Affairs. Outraged by this act, the *Haganah* launched a campaign against both the Sternists and the *Irgun*. While he was fighting the British and other Jews, Begin organized a powerful underground force in the belief that the *Haganah* would eventually join him in attacking the British. In 1945 a united Jewish resistance movement was created which embraced the various Jewish military forces, and on 31 October it began blowing up railways.

In the ensuing years, the campaign against the British continued. In April 1947 after three members of the Irgun were convicted and hanged for destroying the Acre prison fortress, Begin ordered that two British sergeants be hanged. Such an act of revenge provoked worldwide condemnation, and anti-Jewish riots took

place throughout Britain. These incidents encouraged
the British to leave Palestine as soon as possible, and also
coincided with the succession of Harry S. Truman as
President of the United States. Sympathetic to the Jewish
cause and anxious for the support of American Jewry in
the 1948 election, Truman pressed for the creation of a
Jewish state. In May 1947 the Palestinan question came
before the United Nations, and a special committee
was authorized to formulate a plan for the future of the
country. The minority recommended a binational state,
but the majority suggested that there be both an Arab
and a Jewish state as well as an international zone in
Jerusalem. On 29 November this recommendation was
endorsed by the General Assembly.

After this decision was taken, the Arabs began to attack
Jewish settlements. Although the Jewish commanders were
determined to repel this assault, their resources were not
considerable compared with the Arab side. The *Haganah*
had 17,600 rifles, 2,700 sten-guns, about 1,000 machine
guns and approximately 20,000–43,000 men. The Arabs,
on the other hand, had a sizeable liberation army as well
as the regular forces of the Arab states. By March 1948
over 1,200 Jews were killed; in April Ben Gurion ordered
the *Haganah* to link the Jewish enclaves and consolidate
as much territory as possible under the United Nations
plan. Jewish forces occupied Haifa, opened up the route
to Tiberias and Galilee, and captured Safed, Jaffa and
Acre.

Hence, despite constant Arab opposition the State of
Israel was created after 2,000 years of exile. Through the
centuries Jews had been persecuted and murdered, yet

in the face of unrelenting Jew-hatred, the nation united in creating a Jewish state in their ancestral home. Out of despair, a new nation was created, and in the Declaration of Independence read out on 14 May 1948 in the Tel Aviv Museum, David Ben Gurion declared that the Zionists' aim had been realized despite overwhelming hardships. In this proclamation, the Jewish people expressed their deepest longings and hopes for the future:

> The Land of Israel was the birthplace of the Jewish people. Here their spiritual, religious and national identity was formed. Here they achieved independence and created a culture of national and universal significance. Here they wrote and gave their Bible to the world.

> Exiled from Palestine, the Jewish people remained faithful to it in all the countries of their dispersion, never ceasing to pray and hope for their return and the restoration of their national freedom.

> Impelled by this historic association, Jews strove throughout the centuries to go back to the land of their fathers and regain their statehood. In recent decades they returned in their masses. They reclaimed the wilderness, revived their language, built cities and villages and established a vigorous and evergrowing community, with its own economic and cultural life. They sought peace yet were prepared to defend themselves. They brought the blessings of progress to all inhabitants of the country.

In the year 1897 the First Zionist Congress, inspired by Theodor Herzl's vision of the Jewish State, proclaimed the right of the Jewish people to national revival in their own country.

This right was acknowledged by the Balfour Declaration of 2 November 1917, and reaffirmed by the Mandate of the League of Nations, which gave explicit international recognition to the historic connection of the Jewish people with Palestine and their right to reconstitute their national home.

The Nazi Holocaust, which engulfed millions of Jews in Europe, proved anew the urgency of the re-establishment of the Jewish State, which would solve the problem of Jewish homelessness by opening the gates to all Jews and lifting the Jewish people to equality in the family of nations ...

On 29 November 1947 the General Assembly of the United Nations adopted a Resolution for the establishment of an independent Jewish State in Palestine, and called upon inhabitants of the country to take such steps as may be necessary on their part to put the plan into effect.

This recognition by the United Nations of the right of the Jewish people to establish their independent state may not be revoked. It is, moreover, the self-evident right of the Jewish people to be a nation, like all other nations, in its own sovereign state.

Accordingly, we, the members of the National Council, representing the Jewish people in Palestine and the Zionist movement of the world, met together in solemn assembly today, the day of the termination of the British Mandate for Palestine and by virtue of the national and historic right of the Jewish people and of the resolution of the General Assembly of the United Nations, hereby proclaim the establishment of the Jewish State in Palestine, to be called Israel.[1]

20

THE HOLOCAUST AND FAITH

The horror of the Holocaust brought about a transformation of Jewish life. Six million Jews lost their lives at the hands of the Nazis. For many Jews this tragedy eclipsed their belief in the God of history. Yet, for others the terrible events of the Nazi era reaffirmed their faith in the God of the Jewish tradition. In the ghettos and the concentration camps, they went to their deaths convinced that God was with them and would rescue the righteous in a future life. Here, as in previous examples, Jew-hatred and murder led to the renewal of religious dedication and loyalty to the Jewish heritage.

THE HOLOCAUST

After the First World War Germany flourished as a federal republic, but the depression of 1930–2 brought about massive unemployment. As a consequence extremist parties gained considerable support forcing the government to rule by presidential decree. After several unsuccessful conservative coalitions, the president appointed the leader of the National Socialist Workers' Party, Adolf Hitler, as chancellor. Once the Nazis gained control of the government, they pursued their racist objectives by curtailing civil liberties. In 1933 all political parties were eliminated; strikes were forbidden; and trade unions were dissolved. The arrest of dissident scholars and scientists was followed by a purge of the party's radicals. During the next few years, Jews were eliminated from the civil service, the legal and medical professions, and cultural and educational institutions.

In September 1935 the Nuremberg Laws made Jews into second-class inhabitants; in 1938 Jewish communal bodies were put under the control of the Gestapo, and Jews were forced to register their property. Later in the year the Nazi party organized an onslaught against German Jews in which murder and confiscation of property occurred. This event known as *Kristallnacht,* was a prelude to the Holocaust which brought about a new stage of modern Jewish history.

With the first phase of war, pressure on Jews in Germany increased. From September 1939 Jews had to be off the streets by 8:00pm; their movements were restricted; they were banned from various types of transport and deprived of the use of the telephone. From December 1939 Jewish rations were cut and Jews were restricted to specific shopping hours. The Nazis' plan for the elimination of the Jews proceeded in stages. Initially thousands of Jews were deported or put into forced labour camps which frequently led to their death. But in 1941 when the invasion of Russia was imminent, rumours began to circulate that Hitler had entrusted Reinhard Heydrich with the preparation of a Final Solution to the Jewish problem.

The first stage of the Nazis' plan for European Jewry had already begun with the invasion of Poland. When the Jewish population was ghettoized into what Hitler referred to as a huge Polish labour camp, a massive work programme was initiated. Here Jews worked all day, seven days a week, dressed in rags and fed on bread, soup and potatoes. This slave labour operation was a form of murder. As deportations took place throughout Europe, rumours constantly circulated about what fate awaited those who travelled eastward. An observer of this event noted:

> There is great unhappiness and fear among the Jews. From everywhere comes the news about the incredible violence against the Jews. They are bringing trainloads of Jews from Czechoslovakia, Germany, and even from various towns and villages … On the way to Belzec people can see horrifying scenes – especially the railwaymen – because the Jews know very well why they are being taken there, and on the journey they are given neither food nor water.[1]

With the invasion of Russia, mobile killing battalions (*Einsatzgruppen*) moved into Russian towns, sought out the rabbi or Jewish council and obtained a list of all Jewish inhabitants. The Jews were then rounded up in marketplaces, crowded into trains, buses and trucks and taken to the woods where mass graves had been dug. They were then machine-gunned to death.

Other methods were also employed by the Nazis. Mobile gas vans were sent to each battalion of the

Einsatzgruppen. Meanwhile these mobile killing operations were being supplemented by the use of fixed centres, the death camps. The first gassing took place in Auschwitz Block II; then work began on Birkenau, the central killing centre in Auschwitz. The first death camp to be completed was Chelmno which started functioning in December 1941. Subsequently Belzec became operational and the building of Sobibor began in March 1942. At the same time Majdanek and Treblinka were transformed into death centres.

In order to function properly, the organization of the death camps had to be highly efficient. After selection, prisoners were taken to the disrobing rooms; simultaneously the ovens were ignited in the crematoria and wood was piled up next to the burning pits. Victims were informed that after showering they would be given their clothing or told they would have warm soup. After handing over their valuables, they were moved in groups divided by sex through the passage to the gas chambers. When the first groups were pushed into the gas chambers, the *Kommandos* were already bringing clothing to the sorting site and packing it for shipment. Lights were turned off, and the executioner, who wore a gas mask, shook Zyklon B crystals into shafts; after 15 minutes all had been killed. Fans were then turned on to clear the gas chamber. The door was then unbolted, and members of the *Sonderkommando* hosed down the corpses and took them out.

A visitor to Belzec described these horrors:

> The train arrives: 200 Ukrainians fling open the doors
> and chase the people out of the waggons with their

leather whips ... Then the procession starts to move ... And so they climb the staircase and then they see it all: mothers with children at their breasts, little naked children, adults, men and women, all naked ... The chambers fill up ... People are treading on each other's toes. 700–800 in an area of 25 square metres ... After 28 minutes only a few are still alive. At last, after 32 minutes, they are all dead. Men from the work detail open the wooden doors from the other side ... The dead stand like basalt pillars pressed together in the chambers. There is no room to fall or even to lean over. Even in death one can tell which are the families. They are holding hands in death and it is difficult to tear them apart to empty the chambers for the next batch. The corpses are thrown out wet with sweat and urine, smeared with excrement and with menstrual blood on their legs ... Two dozen dentists open mouths with hooks and look for gold. Some of the workers check genitals and anus for gold, diamonds and valuables.[2]

Paradoxically this onslaught against the Jewish people, like the examples we have surveyed, evoked a religious response from many victims. In *The Lights of Faith and Heroism in the Holocaust*, the Orthodox writer Nissim Nasdav observed:

Unquestioning acceptance of the underlying cause of the Holocaust does not exempt us from learning the facts of the Holocaust. A study of the memoirs and testimonies by Jews in the Holocaust is likely to upset accepted conceptions in our understanding of this terrible period ... Observant Jews provided an outstanding example of the aspiration to realize Jewish life even under the greatest duress. The attempt to maintain Torah observance was extremely difficult and was fraught with danger, since observant Jews were the first to be killed by the Germans, who regarded them as the backbone of the Jewish people ...

The experience of *Kiddush ha-Shem*, in the broad sense of the realization of expressly Jewish life, left its mark on the behaviour of many Jews. They desired to live and die as their religious way of life demanded of them, by sanctifying the divine name through the fulfilment of the commandment of *Kiddush ha-Hayyim*. They consciously went to their deaths, with heads held high, as Jews and as humans, in complete contrast to the manner in which the Nazis sought to portray them to themselves and to others ...

There are innumerable examples of religious heroism in the Holocaust, even at the entrances of the gas chambers ... It was a Saturday afternoon. A large number of Jews had been assembled at the train station, to be transported to Auschwitz, where most would be put to death immediately. When they realized that it was time for *seudah shalishit* (the third sabbath meal), the Jews searched for a bit of water and bread, washed their hands, recited the blessing over the bread, and began to sing songs for *seudah shalishit*.

A second instance: a group of fifty young men were brought into the hall where they undressed before the 'showers.' While in this hall, they said to one another: 'Today is Simhat Torah. Let us celebrate the holiday before we die. We have no Torah scroll, but the Holy One, blessed be he, is with us – let us rejoice with him.' They began the traditional dancing and singing, with great fervour ...[3]

For such faithful Jews, the desire to live, and thereby frustrate the plans of the Nazis, was responsible for the survival of many. Such a resolve to live is expressed in the poems written in the ghettos and the extermination camps. An example is a poem written in the Thereisenstadt camp:

> Typhus, like a serpent, chokes the girl.
> Father is bent over, his heart beats once.
> Mother covers her face with her hands
> and we stand, confused
> But we cling to this world,
> Struggling with our last powers against our suffering
> Not to die, but live we are commanded,
> To live, to live, in the name of God. [4]

Jews in the Holocaust sanctified the divine name by such a choice of life. If they had committed suicide instead, they would have presented the Nazis with a victory – instead, they aspired to upset the Nazis' plan by choosing to live rather than die.

For some Jews, the Holocaust has been seen as a

source of hope. In 'Manifestation of Divine Providence in the Gloom of the Holocaust', the Orthodox scholar Hayyim Kanfo explains:

> The Holocaust constitutes the darkness and terrible absence that will cause the events of salvation to spring forth. The previous condition of the Jewish people – the debasement of the diaspora and the severance from Eretz Israel – was excised, so that a new, fresh shoot for which we hope may come forth: the shoot that will constitute the foundation for the restoration of the Davidic line and the return of the Divine Presence to Zion.[5]

Again, in 'Hester Panim in the Holocaust versus the Manifest Miracles in our Generation', Sh'ar Yashuv Cohen, the Chief Rabbi of Haifa, wrote:

> The instinctive and spontaneous response of the myriads who walked to the gas chambers singing 'I believe with perfect faith in the coming of the Messiah' assaults our sensibilities, but it issued from the profound awareness that they were living in the generation of the birth pangs of the Messiah, who will bring the redemption after these tribulations.[6]

Yassel Rakover was a pious Jew who died in the Warsaw ghetto. Although he did not leave any written record, Zvi Kolitz composed a reconstruction of his final reflections. This account symbolizes the faith of many who faced destruction and death at the hands of the Germans:

Death can wait no longer. From the floors above me, the firing becomes weaker by the minute. The last defenders of this stronghold are now falling, and with them falls and perishes the great, beautiful and God-fearing Jewish part of Warsaw. The sun is about to set, and I thank God that I will never see it again. Fire lights my small window, and the bit of sky that I can see is flooded with red like a waterfall of blood. In about an hour at the most I will be with the rest of my family and with millions of other stricken members of my people in that better world where there are no more questions ... Eternally praised be the God of the death, the God of vengeance, of truth and of law, who will soon show his face to the world again and shake its foundations with his almighty voice.[7]

Here in these religious reflections on the Holocaust is a further example of the ways in which Jewish tragedy has given rise to hope and confidence in the future. In the face of persecution and mass murder, Jews went to their deaths confident that God was with them. The paradox of anti-Semitism is that Jew-hatred has repeatedly led to the renewal of faith and the commitment to survive.

Conclusion

These historical examples – stretching back to biblical times – illustrate that Jew-hatred and Jewish survival are interrelated. It is a paradox that Jews need enemies in order to survive. In the past ultra-Orthodox Jewish leaders were profoundly aware of this dynamic. At the beginning of the nineteenth century, for example, Napoleon was battling the Czar for the control of the Pale of Settlement where millions of Jews were compelled to live in poverty. A victory for Napoleon held the promise of freedom and prosperity, first-class citizenship, freedom of movement and an end to persecution. A victory for the Czar, however, would keep the Jews enslaved. The great Hasidic rabbi, Shneur Zalman, stood up in the synagogue on *Rosh Hashanah* to offer a prayer to God asking for help for the leader whose victory would be best for Jewry. He prayed for the Czar to defeat Napoleon. Later he explained: 'Should Napoleon win, the wealth of the Jews will be increased and their position will be raised. At the same time their hearts will be estranged from our Heavenly Father. However, should Czar Alexander win, the Jewish hearts will draw nearer to our Heavenly Father, though the poverty of Israel may become greater and his position lower.'

In recent times the great Eastern European rabbi, Elchanan Wasserman, the dean of a distinguished rabbinical college in Poland, was invited during the Nazi period to bring his students and faculty to Yeshiva College in New York or to the Beis Medrish Letorah in Chicago. He declined this invitation because he believed they are both places of spiritual danger. He reasoned, 'What would one gain to escape physical danger in order to then confront spiritual danger?'. Later, he and his students were murdered by the Nazis. As he was being taken to his death, he reportedly said: 'The fire which will consume our bodies will be the fire through which the people of Israel will arise to a new life.' Theodor Herzl, too, believed that Jew-haters have made us one. 'It is only pressure', he stated, 'that forces us back to the parent stem.' He warned that if our Christian hosts were to leave us in peace for two generations, the Jewish people would merge entirely into surrounding races.

As we have seen, throughout their history Jews have seen themselves as God's suffering servant: for nearly 4,000 years they have remained dedicated to him and to his word. According to the Hebrew Bible, the Jewish people endured hardship at the hands of the Egyptians. Yet despite such contempt, they forged their religious identity during 40 years of wandering in the desert, received the law on Mount Sinai, and eventually entered the land promised to their forefathers. There they built the temple and flourished as a nation state. These events are recorded in the *Haggadah* where God is depicted as the saviour of his people. The symbols used during the Passover *seder* emphasize the misfortunes of the Jewish nation, and their triumph over despair. Pharaoh's actions are portrayed as a paradigm of all efforts by Israel's enemies to overwhelm the Jewish people.

In the ensuing centuries, Jews were similarly oppressed by their surrounding neighbours. In the eighth century BCE the northern kingdom was conquered by the Assyrians; this was followed two centuries later by the Babylonian conquest of the kingdom of Judah. Ancient Israelites were taken to Babylonia where they bewailed their fate; the book of Lamentations expresses their grief and longing to return to Jerusalem. Yet, the people were not overcome by gloom: inspired by the post-exilic prophets, they believed that eventually they would be restored in their ancient homeland. Prophets like Second Isaiah offered them comfort and confidence in the future. By the end of the sixth century, Cyrus the Great decreed that Jews should be allowed to return to Judah and rebuild the temple. Under the leadership of Ezra and Nehemiah, the returning exiles restored the cult and revitalized Jewish life in *Eretz Israel*.

The theme of victory over despair is also a central motif of the festival of *Purim* which allegedly describes events that took place in the fifth century BCE. Even though the dating of this book is disputed, it reflects attitudes towards Jews during the Second Temple period. According to the book of Esther, Haman's plans to destroy the Jewish nation were overcome through the intervention of Esther who pleaded with the king. Haman was then hanged, and these events are celebrated during *Purim* when the book of Esther is read in the synagogue. In mythological terms, Haman personifies all enemies of the Jews who have sought to destroy them.

A further ancient example concerns the triumph of the Maccabees in the second century BCE. During the reign of the Seleucids, Antiochus IV invaded the temple in Jerusalem. He banned circumcision, sabbath observance and the reading of the *Torah*; in addition, he decreed that the temple should be dedicated to the worship of Zeus, and that pigs should be sacrificed on the altar. Such desecration led to a Jewish revolt championed by a priest Mattathias and his sons. They engaged in armed revolt and drove the Seleucids from Jerusalem. During the festival of *Hanukkah*, their victory is celebrated for eight days. Here is a further example of the ways in which the Jewish people were able to triumph over tragedy.

In the first century CE, the temple was destroyed by the Romans following the Jewish revolt. This event marked the end of the Jewish nation, and for 20 centuries the Jewish people were forced to live in exile. Yet despite the destruction of their holy city, the Jewish people continued to worship in synagogues and follow their religious customs. The Pharisees became the dominant religious group, and in the town of Javneh a group of scholars assembled to continue the development of their legal tradition. Through sustained study, scholars collectively reached decisions which were binding on the Jewish populace. Eventually the opinions of these sages were recorded in the *Mishnah* which consists of discussions and rulings of scholars whose teachings had been passed on orally. By the first half of the fourth century, Jewish scholars in *Eretz Israel* collected together the teachings of generations of scholars in Palestine – these discussions of the *Mishnah* became known as the Palestinian *Talmud*. Similarly, in Babylonia the Babylonian *Talmud* was compiled in the sixth century by Rav Ashi. These two works bear testimony to the creative capacity of the Jewish people to survive and prosper through adversity. Despite the tragedy of the Roman conquest, Jewish life flourished under rabbinic leadership.

With the emergence of Christianity, Jewry faced further threats. The emergence of Christian anti-Semitism threatened both Judaism and the Jewish nation. Following New Testament teaching, the early Church fathers condemned Jews for causing Jesus' death. In their view, prophetic denunciations in the Bible against iniquity apply to the Jewish people. Scripture, they argued, bears witness to their iniquity. Jews, they stated, are the enemies referred to in the psalms. They are a dissolute and venomous people who are the source of evil. The Christian assault on the Jewish community had a profound impact on Jewish life. By the fifth century, the status of Jews was transformed. According to Church teaching, the Jew represents Satan; he is an unbeliever, subject to God's wrath. Despite such condemnation, Jews living in Christian lands prospered and the community produced leading rabbinic scholars. Again, out of tragedy, the nation arose and flourished.

The tradition of anti-Semitism created by the early fathers of the Church continued into the Middle Ages. The Jewish population was accused of murdering Christian children, defaming the host, and blaspheming against the Christian faith in the *Talmud*. As Christians embarked on the crusades, they attacked Jewish communities, intent on causing devastation against the enemies of the Christian faith. Throughout the Middle Ages the stereotype of the demonic Jew became a central feature of Christian teaching. Hated by Gentiles, the Jewish community turned inwards and formed their own closed world. Rather than collapse in the face of Jew-hatred, Jews flourished under oppression. Mystical and philosophical speculation reached new heights during this period as did rabbinic scholarship.

Christian hostility against Jewry persisted in the fourteenth century with the Spanish Inquisition. Jews who had converted to Christianity but were suspected of living secretly as Jews were subject to the most terrible ordeals. Tens of thousands suffered the death penalty. Many *conversos* were haunted by self-reproach for converting to Christianity and in their prayers sought forgiveness. Others attempted to de-Christianize themselves. In an attempt to escape the Inquisition, some Jews sought refuge in Portugal and elsewhere where they lived openly as Jews. In these farflung communities, Marranos remained faithful to their Jewish heritage despite the terrors they and their families had endured.

In the early modern period, Jew-hatred continued in Christian lands. Although Jews had prospered in Poland, the mid-seventeenth century witnessed the most terrible onslaught against the Jewish populace. Despite this devastation, the Chmielnicki massacre revived hopes for the coming of the Messiah who would lead his people back to the Holy Land and restore the Jewish nation. When Shabbatai Zevi announced his messiahship, Jews were hysterical, believing that they were living in the final days. When Shabbatai travelled to Constantinople in 1666, his prison quarters became a messianic court. These messianic expectations, however, were crushed when Shabbatai converted to Islam. Inevitably, these events led to widespread disillusionment with the notion of messianic redemption, but this did not diminish the Jewish longing for the creation of a better world. Jewish suffering thus served as the prelude to renewal.

In the modern period, a number of Jewish thinkers were preoccupied with the problem of anti-Semitism. In their view, Jew-hatred is inevitable. According to such thinkers as Moses Hess, Leon Pinsker and Theodor Herzl, Jews will always be viewed as aliens. In their view, Jews are like a nation long since dead. Prejudice against Jews has become rooted and naturalized among all peoples. Such Jew-hatred has given rise to various charges against the Jewish people including drinking the blood of Christians, poisoning wells, exacting usury and defaming the host. Any struggle against this perception is fruitless: Jews will always be viewed as aliens. The only solution, they argued, is for Jews to create a state of their own. In *The Jewish State*, Herzl argued that the creation of a Jewish homeland is a realistic proposal arising out of appalling conditions in Europe. Again, Jew-hatred and Jewish survival were dynamically linked in the quest to protect Jews from danger. In this quest, Arab hostility to Jews living in Palestine intensified Jewish determination to create the State of Israel in their ancestral homeland.

Nazi Germany, too, offers a further example of Jewish loyalty. Under the most terrible conditions, pious Jews retained their faith. Hundreds of thousands of Jews caught up in the Holocaust observed the *mitzvot*. This commitment to the legal tradition enabled these individuals to remain faithful to God. By observing the commandments, they were able to bring a semblance of meaning and sanctity into their lives. Some of these Jews attempted to justify God's providential plan; others related the Holocaust to the suffering prior to the coming of the Messiah; another response focused on the sanctification of God in life in defiance of the Nazi aim to exterminate the Jewish population.

These varied examples demonstrate that hatred of Jews can be a positive force in Jewish history. In all these cases, Jewish existence prospered under the most adverse conditions. Anti-Semitism and Jewish survival are thus intrinsically interconnected. All this is in contrast to the situation of Jews today. As we have seen, the Enlightenment brought about the most dramatic transformation of Jewish life. No longer are Jews confined to the ghettos; instead, the twenty-first century has witnessed the complete integration of Jewry into mainstream society. This revolution, however, has led to the disintegration of traditional Judaism. In place of a unified tradition based on shared belief and practice, modern Jews are deeply divided over the central tenets of the faith, and many have simply cut themselves off altogether from the Jewish heritage. In the absence of Jew-hatred, Judaism is undergoing a slow death. Of course anti-Semitism is an evil – it should be resisted whatever its form. Yet in our increasingly secular and scientific age, we need to acknowledge its paradoxical power to renew and enrich Jewish life.

NOTES

CHAPTER 1

1. Joseph Hertz, *The Authorized Daily Prayerbook* (New York: Bloch, 1948), pp. 249–55.
2. Louis Jacobs, *Principles of the Jewish Faith* (Northvale, NJ: Jason Aronson, 1988), p. 14.
3. Jacobs, *Principles of the Jewish Faith*, p. 15.
4. Jacobs, *Principles of the Jewish Faith*, p. 135.
5. Mishnah, 'Sayings of the Fathers', 1:1.
6. Solomon Ganzfried, *Code of Jewish Law* (New York: Hebrew Publishing Co., 1961), pp. 5–8.
7. Dan and Lavinia Cohn-Sherbok, *The American Jew* (London: HarperCollins, 1994), pp. 104–5.

CHAPTER 2

1. *Encyclopedia Judaica*, vol. 3. (Jerusalem: Keter, 1971), p. 106.
2. *Encyclopedia Judaica*, 3:106.
3. Leon Poliakov, *The History of Antisemitism*, vol 1. (London: Elek Books, 1965), p. 181.
4. Poliakov, *History of Antisemitism*, 1:192–3.
5. Poliakov, *History of Antisemitism*, 1:194.
6. Poliakov, *History of Antisemitism*, 1:279.

CHAPTER 3

1. Wilhelm Christian Dohm, 'Concerning the Amelioration
    of the Civil Status of Jews' in Dan and Lavinia Cohn-
    Sherbok, *A Short Reader of Judaism* (Oxford: Oneworld,
    1997), p. 127.
2. Edict of Joseph II in Cohn-Sherbok, *A Short Reader of
    Judaism*, p. 128.
3. Record of the Assembly of Jewish Notables in Cohn-
    Sherbok, *A Short Reader of Judaism*, p. 128.
4. Dan Cohn-Sherbok, *The Crucified Jew* (Grand Rapids,
    MI:HarperCollins, 1992), pp. 150–1.
5. Heinrich Heine, 'Germany' in Cohn-Sherbok, *A Short
    Reader of Judaism*, p. 129.

CHAPTER 4

1. Moses Mendelssohn, 'Jerusalem' in Dan and Lavinia
    Cohn-Sherbok, *A Short Reader of Judaism* (Oxford:
    Oneworld, 1997), p. 130.

CHAPTER 5

1. Samson Raphael Hirsch, 'Religion Allied to Progress' in
    Paul Mendes-Flohr and Jehuda Reinharz (eds), *The Jew in
    the Modern World* (Oxford: OUP, 1995), p. 200.
2. 'Pittsburgh Platform' in Dan and Lavinia Cohn-Sherbok,
    A Short Reader of Judaism (Oxford: Oneworld, 1997),
    pp. 135–6.
3. Dan Cohn-Sherbok, *Modern Judaism* (London: Macmillan,
    1996), p. 84.
4. Cohn-Sherbok, *Modern Judaism*, p. 84.

5. M. L. Raphael, *Profiles in American Judaism* (New York: Harper and Row, 1984), p. 58.

6. Raphael, *Profiles in American Judaism*, p. 59.

7. Cohn-Sherbok, *Modern Judaism*, p. 92.

8. CCAR, http://ccarnet.org/Articles/index.cfm?id=45&pge _prg_id=1656.

9. CCAR.

CHAPTER 7

1. Dan and Lavinia Cohn-Sherbok, *The American Jew* (London: HarperCollins, 1994), p. 65.

CHAPTER 8

1. Dan Cohn-Sherbok, *Modern Judaism* (London:Macmillan, 1996) p. 156.

2. Cohn-Sherbok, *Modern Judaism*, p. 157.

3. *Guide to Humanistic Judaism* (1993), p. 70.

4. *Guide to Humanistic Judaism* (1993), p. 70.

CHAPTER 9

1. Dan and Lavinia Cohn-Sherbok, *The American Jew* (London: HarperCollins, 1994), pp. 196–8.

2. Cohn-Sherbok, *The American Jew*, pp. 246.

3. Cohn-Sherbok, *The American Jew*, pp. 239–42.

4. Cohn-Sherbok, *The American Jew*, pp. 242.

5. Cohn-Sherbok, *The American Jew*, p. 277.

6. Cohn-Sherbok, *The American Jew*, p. 340.

7. Cohn-Sherbok, *The American Jew*, pp. 303–5.

8. Cohn-Sherbok, *The American Jew*, pp. 315–17.

9. Cohn-Sherbok, *The American Jew*, pp. 312–13.

10. Cohn-Sherbok, *The American Jew*, pp. 242–3.
11. Cohn-Sherbok, *The American Jew*, pp. 242–4.

CHAPTER 10

1. Meir Kahane, *Why Be Jewish?* (New York: Stein and Day, 1983), p. 17.
2. Kahane, *Why Be Jewish*, p. 38.
3. Louis Jacobs, *Principles of the Jewish Faith* (Northvale, NJ: Jason Aronson, 1988), p. 364.
4. Solomon Freehof, *Reform Responses for Our Time* (Cincinnati, OH: HUC Press, 1977), pp. 22–3.

CHAPTER 15

1. Leon Poliakov, *The History of Antisemitism,* vol. 1. (London: Elek Books, 1965), p. 59.
2. Poliakov, *History of Antisemitism*, 1:64.
3. Jacob R. Marcus, *The Jewish in the Medieval World* (New York: Athenaeum, 1977), pp. 115–17.

CHAPTER 16

1. Dan Cohn-Sherbok, *Antisemitism* (Gloucestershire: Sutton, 2002), p. 103.

CHAPTER 17

1. Dan Cohn-Sherbok, *Antisemitism* (Gloucestershire: Sutton, 2002), p. 134.
2. Dan and Lavinia Cohn-Sherbok, *A Short Reader of Judaism* (Oxford: Oneworld, 1997), pp. 110–11.

3. A. Hertzberg (ed.), *The Zionist Idea: A Historical Analysis and Reader* (New York: Athenaeum, 1959), p. 191.

CHAPTER 18

1. A. Hertzberg (ed.), *The Zionist Idea: A Historical Analysis and Reader* (New York: Athenaeum, 1959), p. 209.
2. Hertzberg, *The Zionist Idea*, pp. 225–6.

CHAPTER 19

1. Paul Mendes-Flohr and Jehuda Reinharz (eds), *The Jew in the Modern World* (Oxford: OUP, 1995), p. 629.

CHAPTER 20

1. Cited in Martin Gilbert, *The Holocaust* (London: Macmillan, 1987), p. 308.
2. Cited in J. Noakes and G. Pridham (eds), *Nazism 1919–1945*, 3 vols (Exeter: Exeter University Press, 1995), pp. 1151–2.
3. Cited in Dan Cohn-Sherbok, *Holocaust Theology: A Reader* (Exeter: Exeter University Press, 2002), pp. 84–5.
4. Cohn-Sherbok, *Holocaust Theology*, p. 88.
5. Cohn-Sherbok, *Holocaust Theology*, pp. 102–3.
6. Cohn-Sherbok, *Holocaust Theology*, p. 100.
7. Cohn-Sherbok, *Holocaust Theology*, pp. 77–8.

Glossary

Aliyah: Jewish immigrant to Palestine
Amidah: Eighteen benedictions
Amoraim: Jewish scholars from the third to sixth centuries CE
Baraitot: Rabbinic tradition not included in the *Mishnah*
Eretz Israel: Land of Israel
Exilarch: Head of Babylonian Jewry
Gaon: Head of Babylonian academy
Gehenna: Hell
Gemara: Commentary on the *Mishnah*
Haganah: Jewish military
Haggadah: Passover prayerbook
Halakhah: Jewish law
Hamentashen: Passover cakes
Hanukkah: Festival of Lights
Hasidei Ashkenaz: Rhineland mystics
Haskalah: Jewish Enlightenment
Havdalah: Ceremony terminating the sabbath
Hazzan: Cantor
Hetman: Leader
Hilluk: differentiation and reconciliation of rabbinic opinions
Kabbalah: Jewish mysticism

Kahal: Jewish community
Kavod: Divine glory
Kehillot: Jewish communities
Kibbutzim: Collective village in Israel
Kiddush ha-Shem: Act of martyrdom
Marrano: Baptized Jews suspected of adhering to Judaism
Maskilim: Followers of the Enlightenment
Mikveh: Jewish ritual bath
Minyan: Jewish quorum
Mishnah: Early rabbinic legal code
Mitzvot: Commandments (singular, **Mitzvah**)
Moshavim: Villages of smallholders
Nasi: President of the *Sanhedrin*
Rosh Hashanah: New Year
Seder: Passover meal
Sefirot: Divine emanations
Seudah Shalishit: Third sabbath meal
Shabbat: Sabbath
Shavuot: Festival of Weeks
Shema: Central prayer of the Jewish liturgy
Shofar: Ram's horn
Shulkhan Arukh: Code of Jewish Law
Simhat Torah: Holy day on which the annual reading of the *Torah* is celebrated
Sukkot: Festival of Booths
Talmud: Name of two collections of discussions of Palestinian and Babylonian scholars from the second to sixth centuries CE
Tannaim: Early rabbinic sage of the first to second centuries CE

Tefillin: Phylacteries

Torah MiSinai: Belief that God revealed the *Torah* to Moses on Mount Sinai

Tosafists: *Talmudic* scholars of the twelfth to fourteenth centuries CE

Yeshiva: Rabbinical academy

Yetzer ha-Ra: Evil inclination

Yetzer ha-Tov: Good inclination

Yom Kippur: Day of Atonement

Further Reading

Almog, Shmuel (ed.), *Antisemitism through the Ages* (Oxford, 1988).

Arendt, Hannah, *Antisemitism* (New York, 1968).

Berger, David (ed.), *History and Hate: The Dimensions of Anti-Semitism* (Philadelphia, 1986).

Blech, Arthur, *Anti-Semitism: The Guilt of Jews and Christians* (New York, 1994).

Chesler, Phyllis, *The New Antisemitism* (New York, 2003).

Cohen, Jeremy, *The Friars and the Jews: Evoluton of Medieval Anti-Judaism* (Ithaca, 1982).

Cohen, Norman, *Warrant for Genocide* (London, 1970).

Cohn-Sherbok, Dan, *The Crucified Jew* (London, 1992).

Curtis, Michael (ed.), *Antisemitism in the Contemporary World* (Boulder, 1986).

Dawidowicz, Lucy, *The War Against the Jews* (New York, 1985).

Dinnerstein, Leonard, *Uneasy at Home: Antisemitism* (New York, 1987).

Ettinger, Shmuel, *Antisemitism in the Modern Age* (Tel Aviv, 1978).

Fein, Helen (ed.), *The Persisting Question: Sociological Perspectives and Social Contexts of Modern Antisemitism* (Berlin, 1987).

Finzi, Roberto, *Anti-Semitism* (Gloucestershire, 1999).

Flannery, Edward, *The Anguish of the Jews* (New York, 1985).

Gager, John, *The Origins of Antisemitism* (Oxford, 1985).

Gerber, David, *Anti-Semitism in American History* (Urbana, 1986).

Gilman, Sander and Katz, Steven (eds), *Anti-Semitism in Times of Crisis* (New York, 1991).

Grosser, Paul, *Anti-Semitism, Causes and Effects* (New York, 1983).

Hay, Malcolm, *The Roots of Christian Anti-Semitism* (New York, 1981).

Hirsch, H. and Spiro, J. D., *Persistent Prejudice: Perspectives on Anti-Semitism* (Fairfax, VA, 1988).

Jaher, Frederic Cople, *A Scapegoat in the New Wilderness: The Origins and Rise of Anti-Semitism in America* (Cambridge, 1994).

Kaufman, John, *Jew Hatred: Anti-Semitism, Anti-Sexuality and Mythology in Christianity* (New York, 2001).

Keith, Graham, *Hatred Without a Cause* (Falmouth, 1997).

Klein, Charlotte, *Anti-Judaism in Christian Theology* (London, 1975).

Langmuir, Gavin, *History, Religion and Antisemitism* (Berkeley, 1990).

Langmuir, Gavin, *Toward a Definition of Anti-Semitism* (Berkeley, 1996).

Levy, Richard (ed.), *Antisemitism in the Modern World: An Anthology of Texts* (Lexington, MA, 1991).

Lewis, Bernard, *Semites and Antisemites: An Inquiry Into Conflict and Prejudice* (New York, 1986).

Littell, Franklin, *Crucifixion of the Jews* (New York, 1975).

Litvinoff, B., *The Burning Bush: Antisemitism and World Jewry* (London, 1989).

Morais, Vamberto, *A Short History of Anti-Semitism* (New York, 1976).

Nicholls, William, *Christian Anti-Semitism* (Northvale, NJ, 1993).

Oberman, Heiko, *The Roots of Antisemitism in the Age of Renaissance and Reformation* (Philadelphia, 1984).

Parkes, James, *Antisemitism* (London, 1963).

Quinley, Harold and Clock, Charles, *Anti-Semitism in America* (New Brunswick, 1983).

Rubenstein, W. D. and H., *Philosemitism* (London, 1999).

Shain, Milton, *Antisemitism* (London, 1998).

Stelman, Lionel, *Paths to Genocide: Anti-Semitism in World History* (Basingstoke, 1998).

Telushkin, Joseph and Prager, Dennis, *Why the Jews: The Reason for Antisemitism* (New York, 1983).

Weinberg, Meyer, *Because They Were Jews: A History of Anti-Semitism* (New York, 1986).

Wistrich, Robert, *Antisemitism: The Longest Hatred* (London, 1991).

INDEX